NO-DRAMA DISCIPLINE WORKBOOK

EXERCISES, ACTIVITIES, AND
PRACTICAL STRATEGIES TO CALM THE CHAOS
AND NURTURE DEVELOPING MINDS

DANIEL J. SIEGEL, M.D.
TINA PAYNE BRYSON, Ph.D.

NEW YORK TIMES BESTSELLING AUTHORS
OF *NO-DRAMA DISCIPLINE & THE WHOLE-BRAIN CHILD*

Published by
PESI Publishing & Media
PESI, Inc
3839 White Ave
Eau Claire, WI 54703

Cover: Misa Erder and Amy Rubenzer
Illustrations by: Tuesday Morning
Layout: Bookmasters & Amy Rubenzer

ISBN: 9781559570732

Printed in the United States of America.

PESI
Publishing
& Media
www.pesipublishing.com

Table of Contents

A Special Message from Dan and Tina:

This book is an invitation to take what you learned in the New York Times bestselling No-Drama Discipline, *and go deeper. We want to help you understand your children and yourself more fully, and to become more intentional about who you are as a parent—especially when your kids are acting in ways you don't like.*

This intentionality is key. The less you discipline on autopilot, and instead work from a set of principles and strategies, the more you can not only reduce the drama in your interactions with your kids, and even decrease the amount of time you spend having to discipline. Along the way, you can give your children important skills—about interacting with others, about handling difficult situations, about dealing with strong emotions and impulses, about understanding themselves—all while strengthening your relationship with them.

The book contains stories, illustrations, reflections, projects, and exercises we've designed to help you think about the ways you interact with your kids. We've kept you—the busy parent (or grandparent or childcare provider or teacher or anyone else who loves a child)—in mind throughout. We don't want to overwhelm you, and when we've given you the chance to write, we've tried to keep it short.

In other words, don't look at anything in this book as an assignment, or an obligation. Just view the various reflections and exercises as additional opportunities to help you think more deeply about your children, yourself, and the way you want your family dynamics to play out.

We're grateful to be a part of your journey.

Dan and Tina

CHAPTER 1

Rethinking Discipline

*The pause between reactive and responsive is the
beginning of choice, intention, and
skillfulness as a parent.*

– No-Drama Discipline

We've all faced moments where our kids' behavior sparked a reaction in us that, afterwards, we weren't so proud of. In between the wonderful moments with our children, there are times that parenting can feel confusing, frustrating, triggering, and frankly, exhausting. When you're feeling flooded and your amygdala is keeping your upstairs brain from functioning as it should, it can seem next to impossible to respond to your child's fourth meltdown of the day with anything but exasperation.

We get it. Sometimes you just need to get through it all and survive a difficult moment. But, since you're reading this workbook, we know you'd also like to be able to do more than that.

At the start of *No-Drama Discipline* we introduced the idea that when it comes to discipline and our children, parents must understand the importance of working from an *intentional philosophy* as well as having a *clear and consistent strategy* for responding to misbehavior. Otherwise, you're much more likely to react inconsistently and disproportionally to even small irritations.

So let's begin by getting clear about what your parenting philosophy is, what strategies you turn to, and how they're working for you and your children. Following, you'll find the four illustrations from the first chapter of *No-Drama Discipline*. In looking over these common parenting responses, consider how closely they resemble your common reaction to discipline issues in your family.

Which illustration resonates with you the most? In the lines below, write about what feels most familiar as you look at these common discipline scenarios.

_____

_____

_____

As you read further, keep scenarios like these in your mind. Think about whether your typical response is more *reactive*, where you go into autopilot and rely on old habits, or *responsive* where you're intentional and make conscious decisions based on an overall parenting philosophy.

Autopilot/Reactiveness	Intentionality/Responsiveness
An automatic response to stimuli without reflection or intention on your part.	Making conscious decisions based on principles you've thought about and agreed upon beforehand.
A reaction to behavior without thought given to what you're trying to teach in the moment.	Considering various options, then choosing the one that engages a thoughtful approach toward the desired outcome.
Can lead to overreaction on parent's part and may result in punishments or "consequences" that don't relate to the behavior in question.	Leads to clear behavioral boundaries and structure, and thus effective teaching, with skill-building in mind.

By taking the time to really look at how you behave in response to your children, you're giving yourself the chance to shift out of autopilot mode. In doing that, you'll be better able to respond in a way that not only stops behavior you don't like in the short term, but also teaches those life skills that ultimately build character and prepare your kids for making good decisions in the future.

THE THREE QUESTIONS: WHY? WHAT? HOW?

One way to increase your ability to respond in a thoughtful and intentional way is to use the why-what-how questions as your go-to response to all of your kids' unwanted behaviors. Let's review, briefly, the meaning behind each of the three questions:

WHY DID MY CHILD ACT THIS WAY?	• Approach with curiosity instead of assumptions. • Look deeper to see what may be behind the behavior. • Assess whether the behavior was developmentally appropriate.
WHAT LESSON DO I WANT TO TEACH IN THIS MOMENT?	• Remember that the goal of discipline isn't about consequences. • Based on the situation, consider what life-skills might need strengthening (*self-control, the importance of sharing, taking responsibility for your actions, appropriate ways to express big feelings, etc.*).
HOW CAN I BEST TEACH THIS LESSON?	• Consider the child's age and developmental stage, as well as the context of the situation. • Take both your own and your child's emotional state into consideration (*i.e.: is she capable of learning now? Are you capable of teaching?*). • Use collaborative problem solving (*you don't need to rescue him, but he may need help thinking through ideas and building the skills needed to solve his own problems*).

INSTEAD OF LECTURING...

ASK THE THREE QUESTIONS

CHOOSING RESPONSIVE OVER REACTIVE

Before we can reflect on these questions, we've got to be in control of ourselves. So before we apply the three questions, let's talk about recognizing what we need in order to stay in—or get back to—the frame of mind needed to respond intentionally when interacting with our kids.

We'll begin by helping you create a go-to list of ideas for remaining in a calm, mindful, intentional state. First, think about tools that can move you from reactive to responsive. These are strategies that can help quickly change your mindset. We've started the list for you. Reflect on what works for you, and add your own below.

Short-Term Tools To Help You Be
Responsive Instead Of Reactive

- *Mentally list 3 things you love about your child before you approach a situation where he is acting out.*
- *Count to ten before responding at all.*
- *Before reacting, breathe in deeply through your nose for a count of five. Hold for a count of five, then slowly exhale through your mouth. Do at least twice if time permits.*
- *Do a quick body scan before reacting. Notice whether you are tensing up or expressing anger physically (i.e.: tight jaw, tense shoulders, etc.). If you feel that tension, do a "wet dog" shake to release pent up emotions before responding. (Start a shake at the top of your head, then continue down through your body by relaxing your facial muscles, shoulders, arms, torso, and so on, down through your legs.)*

- _____

- _____

- _____

Now compile a similar list of long-term tools, methods that build your mindfulness habit over time and help you remain calm.

Long-Term Tools To Help You Be
Responsive Instead Of Reactive

- *Self-care: Make sure you're getting sleep, exercising, and having fun in your own life. ("If Momma or Daddy ain't happy, ain't nobody happy.")*
- *Take a few minutes each morning before fully waking up to mentally "create" your day: In your mind, visualize your day going smoothly as you respond intentionally to your children's needs.*
- *Make a visual representation of your parenting goals (peaceful family meals, vacations, easy bedtime routine…) and place it where you'll see it each day.*

- *Write reminders and quotes from this book and others on sticky notes and place them on your steering wheel, refrigerator, bathroom mirror, and anywhere else you'll be, to help remind yourself about how you want to think about and be with your kids.*

- _____

- _____

APPLYING THE THREE QUESTIONS

Now that you've got some tools ready for the next time your kids' behaviors challenge you to be responsive rather than reactive, let's put the questions into practice. Remember, you want to avoid disciplining on autopilot:

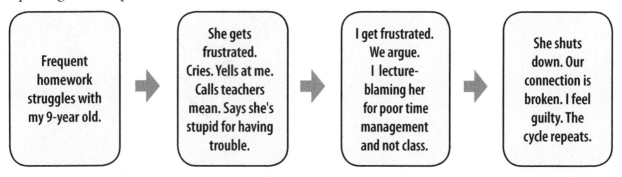

As you can see, reacting without thinking things through rarely results in an outcome you want. In times like these, because you're just reacting, you're unable to consider what your child really needs in the moment. Thus, you lose the opportunity to offer real guidance that can ultimately break the cycle of unwanted behavior and lead to her emotional and intellectual growth.

Alternately, let's consider what could happen in the same situation when the parent responds intentionally, using the three questions:

WHY DID MY CHILD ACT THIS WAY?	• Homework is a constant struggle. Maybe she feels frustrated. • Perhaps there's something her homework that feels overwhelming to her • Does she feel tired? Sick? Hungry? • Did she have a bad day today? Maybe there are outside circumstances that have put her into this mood today.
WHAT LESSON DO I WANT TO TEACH IN THIS MOMENT?	• Effective time management? • Responsibility? • Handling frustration well? • Making good choices about activities outside of school?
HOW CAN I BEST TEACH THIS LESSON?	• Is this a teachable moment? Are we both in a receptive state of mind? Should I help or soothe first, talk later? • Ask questions and problem-solve together so she's involved in coming up with solution for the homework dilemma. • Take this as an opportunity to collaborate on strengthening our relationship as well as improving the homework experience.

INSTEAD OF JUST REACTING...

ASK THE THREE QUESTIONS

It may seem, at first glance, that this would all take too much time when you've got a potential meltdown brewing. However, what you'll find is that the more you practice the three questions, the quicker you'll understand the motivations behind your kids' behaviors. And the more you understand your children, the stronger your connection grows, and the more weight your advice and guidance has.

All the more reason to start your practice now! Let's try using the three questions with a few recent disciplinary interactions that happened within your own family. Begin by describing a particular situation and detail your child's behaviors (*comments, body language, facial expressions, emotions...*) in the space below.

EVENT

Regardless of how you may have responded or reacted to the situation at the time, in order to come up with as many potential answers to each of the three questions as you can, take a few moments now to think about:

- **What you know about your child's temperament** (*Is he a perfectionist? Does she keep her emotions bottled up? Is it important to him to make others proud? Does she tend to get easily overwhelmed? ...*)
- **What you recall about the events leading up to the specific interaction** (*Was it a very busy day with many unexpected changes? Were there any exchanges with other children at school that could have set him on edge? Did she have enough sleep the night before? ...*)
- **How your child tends to learn best** (*Is he primarily a visual learner? Does she need to experience things in order to retain information? Is he an auditory learner - responding well to dialogue and discussion? Does she understand the gestalt of the situation? Is she more of a "black and white" thinker? ...*)

Keeping these ideas in mind, write your answers to the three questions:

1. Why did my child act this way?

   _____

   _____

   _____

   _____

2. What do I want to teach in this moment?

_____

_____

_____

_____

3. How can I best teach this lesson?

_____

_____

_____

_____

You may have noticed that often you respond to a situation from *your* state of mind, as opposed to what your child needs at that particular time. The three questions help us remember who our individual child is and what her unique needs are in that moment in time. Remember: don't think of discipline as an one-size-fits-all solution. Instead, *remember how important it is to discipline (teach) this one child in this one moment.*

CAN'T VS. WON'T

When it comes to discipline, one of the most important distinctions is the one between what a child *can't* do, and what a child *won't* do. Kids who fail to behave as they're expected to are often seen as being willfully disobedient, as just *deciding* to be difficult. But the truth is that sometimes it's not that they *won't* control themselves and make good decisions, but that they *can't*. Children, just like adults, have a fluctuating capacity to handle what's thrown at them.

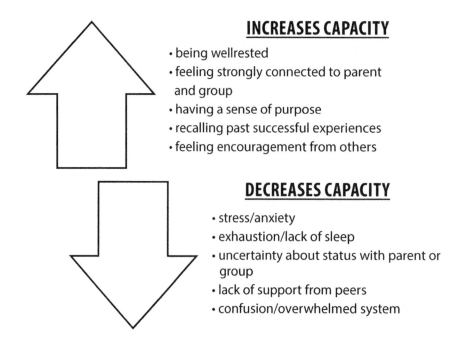

INCREASES CAPACITY

- being wellrested
- feeling strongly connected to parent and group
- having a sense of purpose
- recalling past successful experiences
- feeling encouragement from others

DECREASES CAPACITY

- stress/anxiety
- exhaustion/lack of sleep
- uncertainty about status with parent or group
- lack of support from peers
- confusion/overwhelmed system

Your child *wants* to be in connection with you. He *wants* to make you proud. He *wants* to be noticed for what he does well, instead of what he does that disappoints you. But, given all of the reasons he might struggle, it's not possible for him to be who he wants to be every time. It's usually the case that if he *could* do better, he would.

Distinguishing Can't From Won't

Let's get some practice distinguishing can't from won't. Begin this exercise by listing in the following chart some unwanted behaviors your child recently exhibited. Next, list any *won'ts*, reasons you have to believe that she just *wouldn't* do what you wanted her to do—even if the only reasons you have are the irrational thoughts that run through your head during moments like this (he's trying to drive me crazy, she is self-centered, he cares more about his friends than his family, etc.). In the next space, write down *can'ts*, reasons she might not have been *able* to do what was expected of her. Dig deep and think of every possible reason – you'll have an opportunity to discount your guesses at the end.

The last blank might be the most important one in this exercise. Look over your "can't do it" and "won't do it" lists carefully. In the far right column you're going to agree with or discount each of your reasons so that you are able to make a choice as to whether you think your child was behaving poorly on purpose or because she couldn't do what was expected of her *in that particular moment, given her developmental stage.*

We've given you two examples to begin, but think about your own children and add as many variations as you can based on recent experiences with your own kids.

BEHAVIOR	Procrastinating for so long over getting dressed today that we were late for school. Again.
WON'T DO IT BECAUSE...	1. She wants to be late for school. 2. She only cares about herself. 3. She's lazy. 4. She wants me to do everything for her.
CAN'T DO IT BECAUSE...	1. She's frustrated because she hasn't learned to button/tie shoes yet? 2. She's worried about her friends teasing her again about her clothes not matching? 3. She's nervous about not having done her homework well and is delaying the inevitable reality of having to turn it in? 4. She hasn't learned how to focus and not get sidetracked by other interests.
CAN'T OR WON'T?	• I know she doesn't really only care about herself, and I know she's actually not lazy – even though I get frustrated sometimes when she won't do things for herself. She wants me to do stuff for her that she can do herself because it helps her feel connected and cared for. • And even though she sometimes can get dressed without a hassle, I know every day is different. • She hasn't been sleeping well a lot and that homework assignment really has her stressed. • She's so sensitive about being made fun of and not having the "cool" clothes makes it hard sometimes. • <u>Decision: Can't</u> In this case, I think she made us late for school because she really couldn't do any better this morning, and my flipping my lid only made her feel worse about herself and raised her reactivity. I'll think through how to be more proactive tomorrow morning and work on some skill-building so she can naturally do better.

BEHAVIOR	Even though it's well past bedtime, he keeps coming up with excuses to call for me.
WON'T DO IT BECAUSE...	1. I can tell he's exhausted, so he has to be doing this on purpose. 2. He listens when I yell – so this will continue unless I am firm with him. 3. No matter what I give him, he keeps asking for something else – so he's obviously pretending.
CAN'T DO IT BECAUSE...	1. Daddy came home right before bed and got him all excited? 2. He needs help to process something that happened that day (fears, stress, sadness...)? 3. I rushed through the bedtime routine because I'm tired and he senses the disconnection and is trying to get more connection? 4. He doesn't want to the day to be over?

CAN'T OR WON'T?	• Even though he's exhausted, the fact that he was watching TV up until his bedtime and then his dad came home and riled him up, could be a reason that he's having trouble settling down.
	• And then I rushed through his bedtime routine so I didn't give him any help with that either.
	• When I get so frustrated that I yell, he does listen. But maybe that's because then he's scared of me, or he gives up on my actually helping him get over whatever he's having trouble with. When I yell at him to go to sleep, it's even harder for him to settle and go to sleep—I'm revving him up even more!
	• <u>Decision: Can't</u> Maybe all he actually wants is a few minutes of really connecting with me before he goes to sleep – that's why he keeps making up excuses to come back out. Maybe he doesn't even know that's what he needs. He's just a little kid. I bet that would make him feel safe and loved and he could let go and sleep after that.

Now choose one of your child's typical behaviors and go through the same process:

BEHAVIOR	
WON'T DO IT BECAUSE...	
CAN'T DO IT BECAUSE...	
CAN'T OR WON'T?	

As you become more aware of how often "acting out" is actually your child showing you that she's having a moment of difficulty managing feelings and behavior and that she needs you or needs to build skills, you'll find yourself trying to come up with better responses than you previously had to that unwanted behavior.

INSTEAD OF A ONE-SIZE-FITS-ALL TIME-OUT...

GIVE THEM PRACTICE MAKING GOOD CHOICES

ONE-SIZE-FITS-ALL DISCIPLINE

Still, despite the many discipline tools at your disposal, at times you'll likely fall back on those old stand-by techniques.

Let's do a quick check-in. Be honest with yourself and mark on the graph below how often you find yourself using one of your old go-to techniques (*yelling, threats, time-outs, spanking, etc.*), rather than disciplining intentionally in the moment.

Never   Sometimes   Often

Next, get specific about your triggers. Write down when you're most likely to use any of these old methods of discipline (*when you're tired/stressed, around your in-laws, in public, when you feel overwhelmed…*).

_____

_____

_____

_____

This list is important because it gives you a clearer indication of what the triggers are that keep you from disciplining in the moment, and where and when you need the most support. We all have times when it's hard for us to be the best version of ourselves. Knowing exactly what makes it more difficult for *you*, gives you the opportunity to find the support that helps you discipline the way you want.

That's what we'd like you to do now. Keeping the trigger list you just created in mind, take a look at the support suggestions we've listed below and on the next page. Circle whichever ones you think would be most helpful when you're faced with a trigger that would usually result in your slipping back into your old discipline methods. Use the space under each idea to make any specific notes about how you'd make this work for yourself (when you would do it, how long you would do it for, who you would call, etc.). This is, by no means, a comprehensive list—feel free to add any additional ideas that could work for you.

- Educate extended family about our parenting/discipline choices/child development

  _____

  _____

- Talk to a therapist/join parenting group

  _____

  _____

- Call a friend

  _____

  _____

- Meditate

  _____

  _____

- Exercise

  _____

  _____

- Ask my partner to take over parenting moments that are hardest for me

  _____

  _____

- Delegate responsibilities *(at home, at work, with the kids...)*

  _____

  _____

- Take breaks from my kids

  _____

  _____

- Additional ideas

  _____

  _____

  _____

  _____

- Work more hours from home

  _____

  _____

- Work less hours from home

  _____

- Arrange for a babysitter and have fun

  _____

  _____

- Give the kids more responsibilities

  _____

  _____

- Eat a more balanced diet/sleep more/ exercise

  _____

  _____

TEMPERAMENT AND SETTING BOUNDARIES

In approaching discipline from this new perspective of making intentional, moment-to-moment decisions, it's still important that you set clear, firm boundaries. Your child needs you to do so.

As you do, keep these points in mind:

- My child's actions are clues to needs not being met, or skills that need strengthening.
- I need a discipline strategy that takes specific circumstances into account.
- My old one-size-fits-all discipline approach (*taking away privileges, time-outs...*) will rarely be effective in teaching my children long-term behavior management skills.

Since we know there isn't one method that works for every child in every situation when it comes to changing behavior, how do you know what approach to take? The best way to begin is to understand your child's individual temperament and behavior clues.

Take a few minutes to think about how your child behaves *most of the time*. When you take her to a birthday party with a bounce house, does she immediately run off to play and jump, or does she cling to your side? When confronted with plans unexpectedly changing, is his natural inclination to go with the flow, or does he get anxious and upset, wanting things to be the way they were promised? The ways in which your child reacts to the world around him are clues to his true personality.

Below, write whatever you can think of that would describe your child's temperament (*curious, cautious, conscientious, extroverted, intellectual, anxious, open, active, etc.*).

_____

_____

_____

Next, go back through this list and cross out words that describe only your child's *temporary* feelings or behaviors that depend on the situation, and don't fit as a core personality trait. For example, *angry* is a temporary state your child is in because of a certain situation (*He's angry because I wouldn't let him stay out late with his friends last night*). In other words, being angry isn't a *trait* – something that is at the core of who he is. Having separated states from traits, the remaining words describe your child's temperament. Write those words here.

My Child's Temperament:

_____

_____

_____

Understanding that some of how kids behave is because of who they are, fundamentally, will help you see how a different approach to discipline might be needed for different children.

CHASE THE WHY

Being curious is another way to snap out of automaticity and reactive behavior. Find a quiet place to sit and think about your child during some of his more difficult episodes and "chase the why." *Why* does he react that way when he loses at a game? *Why* did she get so frustrated when I said no? *Why* is it so hard for him to do his chores in the morning?

The more we understand the reasons *behind* our children's behaviors, the less likely we'll be to react from a place of anger and frustration when they do something we don't like. And the more we're able to respond intentionally, the quicker our children will be to make lasting positive changes in the way they behave.

In the first section of the following chart, list a common behavior struggle you have with your child. Next chase the why, then see how it might affect your response to that behavior. Use our example as a guide, then come up with a couple of examples of your own.

BEHAVIOR/CONTEXT	5-year old throwing tantrum at dinnertime. Context • Eating dinner later than usual • At Grandma's house • Lots of extended family – all adults • Only child • A sensitive and very physical kid
CHASING THE WHY	Questioning the behavior: Maybe the chaos of so many people around at dinnertime made him overwhelmed—he's not used to that. He also was stuck in the house with a lot of grownups and couldn't run around as much as he usually does at home. He probably was dysregulated because dinner was late, so that made him even more out of sorts. I think what finally pushed him over the edge was that he thought he was having his favorite dinner, but Grandma "surprised him" with something else. We were asking him to sit for a long time.
ALTERNATIVE RESPONSE	Response: Normally I might give him a time-out, or not let him have dessert, because of his behavior at the table. But, thinking about <u>why</u> he ended up getting so upset makes me think that a better way to respond would have been to: • First, help him calm down by empathizing with him. • Next, remove him from the chaotic environment – but stay with him while he regulates. • Let him get some of his energy out, if he wants to, by wrestling a little. • Since he's only 5, I think helping him process what happened (putting words to why he was feeling they way he did) would be most helpful. • Once he's calmed down and feeling our connection again, I can explain why his behavior wasn't the best way to show what he needed. I would ask him if there's anything he'd like to say or do for Grandma. Because he's so sensitive he might want to tell her that he's sorry, but maybe not in front of everyone else. Together, he and I can decide if he wants to dictate a note to her, or if he wants to say anything to her privately.

BEHAVIOR/CONTEXT	

CHASING THE WHY	
ALTERNATIVE RESPONSE	

BEHAVIOR/CONTEXT	
CHASING THE WHY	
ALTERNATIVE RESPONSE	

Keep in mind, this is not the same as being indulgent or catering to your children at every turn. As we said before, boundaries and limits are important. They make a child safe, and help him understand the way the world works. The difference here is that including an understanding of what each individual child is capable of *in the moment* allows you to tailor your discipline approach in such a way that you've increased the effectiveness of teaching those limits and boundaries—ultimately leading to experiencing fewer and fewer moments of off-track behavior.

DEFINING YOUR DISCIPLINE PHILOSOPHY

The main goal of this chapter, as a whole, has been to help you make the move from habitual reactions and a one-size-fits-all discipline approach, to thought-out principles and strategies that both match your belief systems and respect your children for who they are as individuals.

Let's close the chapter by allowing you to reflect on how well you think you're doing on this already. How intentional are you when you discipline your children? Using the space below, explore these questions for yourself, paying attention to how you feel as you answer each question.

- *Do I have a discipline philosophy?* How purposeful and consistent am I when I don't like how my kids are behaving?

_____

_____

_____

_____

- *Is what I'm doing working?* Does my approach allow me to respectfully teach my kids the lesson I want to teach, in terms of both immediate behavior and how they grow and develop as human beings? And am I finding that I need to address behaviors less and less, or am I having to discipline about the same behaviors over and over?

_____

_____

_____

_____

- *Do I feel good about what I'm doing?* Does my discipline approach help me enjoy my relationship with my children more? Do I usually reflect on discipline moments and feel pleased with how I handled myself? Do I frequently wonder if there's a better way?

_____

_____

_____

_____

- *Do my kids feel good about it?* Discipline is rarely going to be popular, but do my children understand my approach and feel my love? Am I communicating and modeling respect in a way that allows them to still feel good about themselves?

_____

_____

_____

_____

_____

- *Do I feel good about the messages I'm communicating to my children?* Are there times I teach lessons I don't want them to internalize. For example, that obeying what I say is more important than learning to make good decisions about doing the right thing? Or that power and control are the best ways to get people to do what we want? Or that I only want to be around them when they're pleasant?

_____

_____

_____

_____

_____

- *How much does my approach resemble that of my parents?* How did my parents discipline me? Can I remember a specific experience of discipline and how it made me feel? Am I just repeating old patterns? Rebelling against them?

_____

_____

_____

_____

_____

- *Does my approach ever lead to my kids apologizing in a sincere manner?* Even though this might not happen on a regular basis, does my approach at least leave the door open for it?

_____

_____

_____

_____

_____

- *Does it allow for me to take responsibility and apologize for my own actions?* How open am I with my kids about the fact that I make mistakes? Am I willing to model for them what it means to own up to one's errors?

_____

_____

_____

_____

_____

An exercise like this one, where you're looking critically at your parenting, can be an intense experience for many people. Because a wide range of emotions can be triggered when you're doing this type of self-reflection, it's helpful to take some time to notice how answering the questions above made you feel. (*For example, did you notice feelings of regret, shame, or guilt? Was there a point where you felt overwhelmed or hopeless? Was there anything that made you proud of yourself or grateful that you had improved something on your own already?*) Bringing that internal dialogue to your consciousness allows you to acknowledge your feelings and work through any uncomfortable emotions you have that might get in the way of making the changes you're after.

Use the space below to reflect on how answering the questions made you feel:

_____

_____

_____

_____

_____

Self-examination isn't always easy to do, so let's acknowledge the courage you've had to tackle these exercises head on. No matter how long you've been parenting, or how many mistakes you think you've made along the way, you should know that you're giving your children an enormous gift by doing this work. It's important to have compassion for yourself and acknowledge that you've done the best you could with the information you had at the time—and as you know better, you do better!

CHAPTER 2

Your Brain on Discipline

*If repeated experiences actually change the physical architecture
of the brain, then it becomes paramount that we be
intentional about the experiences we give our children.*

— No-Drama Discipline

Research has shown that the way we interact with our kids when they're upset significantly affects how their brains develop, and therefore what kind of people they are, both today and in the years to come. Having even a basic level of understanding of the neuroscientific concepts discussed in this chapter can completely change the way you understand and relate with your children—allowing you to interact with them more enjoyably, and when it's necessary, to discipline them more effectively and with less drama.

THE THREE BRAIN C'S

Let's begin by applying the "Brain C's" and look at how they can impact your disciplinary decisions when your kids lose control of their behavior.

BRAIN C #1 — THE BRAIN IS CHANGING

The first Brain C reminds us that the upstairs part of the brain that controls more sophisticated thinking – emotional regulation, sound decision making, empathy, morality, etc. – is not fully formed until a person reaches their mid-twenties. As a result, *our expectations of what our children are capable of must be tempered.*

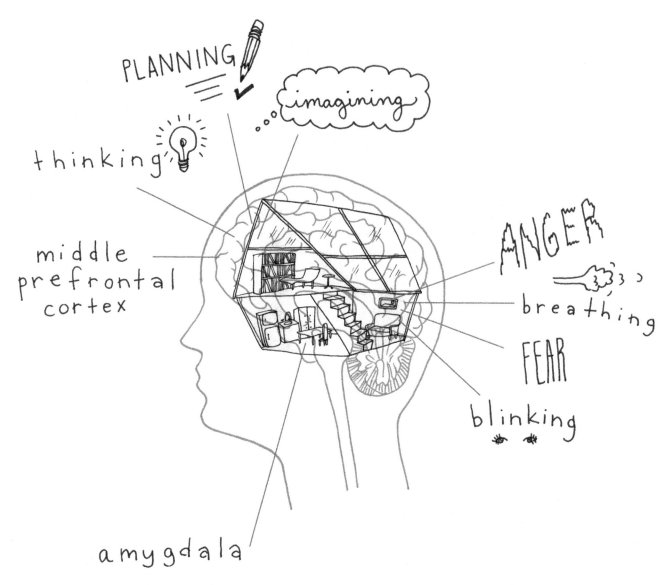

Think about what that means practically: our kids are working with an upstairs brain that isn't yet fully formed. And the part that *is* fully formed, the downstairs brain—which is supposed to detect and react to threats instantly and impulsively—does so without thought or careful planning. Guess which part of the brain is going to become the default when things go wrong!

And yet, as parents we so often expect our kids to make decisions and respond to the world as *we* do: as adults with fully formed, fully functioning brains.

It's possible that you're not even aware of how much you do this, or in what areas you place those expectations on your children. But, if you find yourself getting frustrated with your children's behavior on a regular basis, it's likely that there are times you're expecting more of them than they're capable of.

Let's take a closer look at how you think your kids should behave. On the next page, you'll find a list of thinking, emotional, and relational skills that a fully formed upstairs brain controls. Each set of skills has a graph underneath it. With 1 being "unable" and 5 being "mastery," circle the point on the graph to indicate how much mastery of each skill you think your child *should* have at this point in his life.

Sound decision making and planning

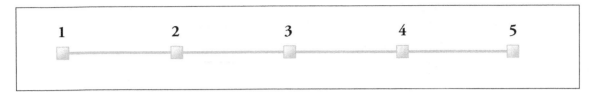

Regulation of emotions and body

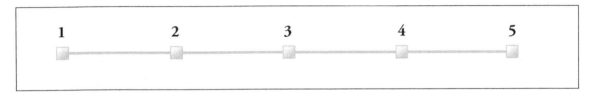

Personal insight

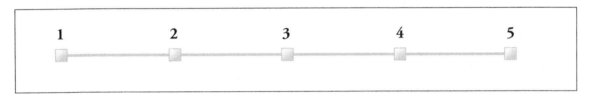

Flexibility and adaptability

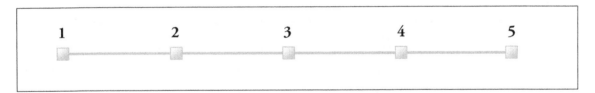

Empathy

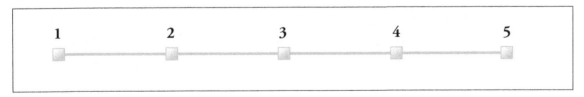

Morality

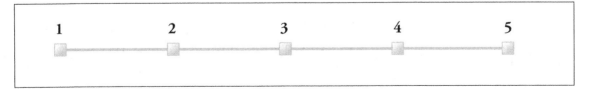

Now let's apply those expectations to your child's behavior. Begin by bringing to mind a recent moment where your child did something inappropriate or behaved in a way you didn't like. Close your eyes and picture the exchange, running through the details in your mind. Now, in the space below, write your description of what happened.

_____

_____

_____

_____

Next, consider how *capable* your child was of connecting to her higher-level thinking. Did she think things through before she acted? Was she able to articulate her feelings? Did she raise her voice or throw something? Did she tell the truth about what happened? Did she consider how her actions might make others feel? Take all of that into consideration and answer the following questions, writing your answers in the space provided.

- In this particular instance, can you detail any examples of the life skills controlled by the upstairs brain—the ones listed above—that your child was less capable of accessing than you expected?

_____

_____

_____

_____

- Can you describe what might have diminished her capacity to control those behaviors this time (feeling overwhelmed, hungry, tired…)?

_____

_____

_____

_____

- When you consider this specific interaction with your child, how closely does the level of mastery you indicated your child *should* have, actually match what you observed?

_____

_____

_____

_____

When we understand the first Brain C, that the brain is changing and hasn't yet fully developed, we can more fully comprehend that we may be expecting too much of our kids. As a result we can deepen the parent-child connection. And we can be more patient as we trust that development is in the works.

Plus, when we use our own mindsight to sense the mind behind our children's behavior—to understand their point of view and how they are feeling, their developmental stage, and what they're ultimately capable of—we can then model the empathy, compassion, and insight we ultimately want our children to have themselves.

BRAIN C #2 — THE BRAIN IS CHANGEABLE

Brain C #2 is all about neuroplasticity - the relatively recent understanding that the brain physically changes based on our experiences. You'll remember from *No-Drama Discipline* that everything our children see, hear, feel, touch, and smell impacts their brain and influences the way they view and interact with their world. What's more is that when an experience, either positive or negative, is repeated over and over, it deepens and strengthens the connections among the neurons in our brain. Neuroscientists express this idea as "neurons that fire together wire together."

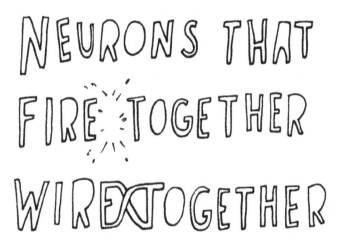

Because we know that repeated experiences actually change our children's brains, we have an even greater incentive to be intentional not only about how we respond to them but also how the other people in our children's lives affect their mental model for relationships.

Think for a minute right now about the important people in your child's life. How do they communicate with her? How do they help her reflect on her actions and behavior? What do they teach her about relationships – about respect, trust, and effort? What opportunities do they expose her to? What associations are they building in her brain?

In order to get clear about this, create a list of all the people your child has regular interactions with (*grandparents, a coach, peers, a teacher…*) and answer the three questions following with respect to each person. We've offered an example to get you started.

Name/Relationship: _Coach O'Rourke/swim coach_

What experiences does my child receive with this person, and how are those experiences affecting my child's brain?

He meets his coach three times weekly in the early mornings. Coach O'Rourke stresses routine, and she's giving my son a strong sense of responsibility and commitment. She also helps him develop his good decision-making skills, as she wants him to be well rested in order to wake on time for practice. Additionally, he is seeing how much Coach cares for him, even as she challenges him to be better.

- Is this relationship producing "healthy" firing and wiring, or does my child seem to be developing some negative associations from the relationship?

  This relationship feels like a good one. Coach is a good role model for him—showing dedication and commitment to the team, as well as to the sport. Coach also treats him with respect, giving constructive criticism and praise in a way that makes my son want to work harder to meet his own goals.

- Do you want to make any changes based on these observations?

  No. At this stage I'm very happy with the relationship he has with Coach O'Rourke. I'm keeping my eyes on things to make sure his time commitment doesn't increase so much that it becomes unbalanced, but so far, so good.

Name/Relationship: _____

- What experiences does my child receive with this person, and how are those experiences affecting my child's brain?

  _____
  _____
  _____
  _____

• Is this relationship producing "healthy" firing and wiring, or does my child seem to be developing some negative associations from the relationship?

_____

_____

_____

_____

• Do you want to make any changes based on these observations?

_____

_____

_____

_____

Name/Relationship: _____

• What experiences does my child receive with this person, and how are those experiences affecting my child's brain?

_____

_____

_____

_____

• Is this relationship producing "healthy" firing and wiring, or does my child seem to be developing some negative associations from the relationship?

_____

_____

_____

_____

• Do you want to make any changes based on these observations?

_____

_____

_____

Name/Relationship: _____

- What experiences does my child receive with this person, and how are those experiences affecting my child's brain?

_____

_____

_____

_____

- Is this relationship producing "healthy" firing and wiring, or does my child seem to be developing some negative associations from the relationship?

_____

_____

_____

_____

- Do you want to make any changes based on these observations?

_____

_____

_____

_____

EXPERIENCE LITERALLY CHANGES THE BRAIN

In addition to the relationships our kids have with others, the activities they're involved in (piano lessons, screen time, community service, free play, etc.) play an equally large role in shaping their brains. Using the same process as you did above, evaluate the benefits of the activities your child engages in—listing them in order of most to least time spent participating. Again, we've offered an example to start with.

(Example) Activity: <u>Screen Time</u>

- What is my child's experience when participating in this activity, and how does that experience affect my child's brain?

  <u>He experiences a sense of belonging because most of his friends play</u>
  <u>video games as well. He also experiences a sense of mastery because</u>
  <u>he's skilled at many of the games. Both of those are pretty healthy</u>
  <u>experiences. However, he also experiences being able to zone out and</u>
  <u>not have to communicate with other people while he's playing, as well</u>
  <u>as staying inside and sitting on the couch instead of going outside to</u>
  <u>play. Neither of those seems like it's affecting his brain in a positive way.</u>

- Is this activity producing "healthy" firing and wiring, or does my child seem to be developing some negative associations from the activity?

  <u>I'm concerned that he only feels competent in his role as "gamer," and</u>
  <u>that it doesn't translate to how he feels at school. The iPad is also</u>
  <u>the first (and only) thing he wants to do when we're at home. There</u>
  <u>seems to be a negative type of firing and wiring happening in that he</u>
  <u>no longer seems able to entertain himself without the screen time—as if</u>
  <u>fun and relaxation only happen if he's attached to it.</u>

- Do you want to make any changes based on these observations?

  <u>Definitely. We need to cut back on the amount of time he is spending on</u>
  <u>video games and screen time. Perhaps we need to try something like</u>
  <u>making sure he does x amount of time being active or creative in order</u>
  <u>to earn some screen time. I'd also like to find a way help him take pride</u>
  <u>in other skills.</u>

Activity: _____

- What is my child's experience when participating in this activity, and how does that experience affect my child's brain?

  _____

  _____

  _____

  _____

  _____

- Is this activity producing "healthy" firing and wiring, or does my child seem to be developing some negative associations from the activity?

  _____

  _____

  _____

  _____

  _____

- Do you want to make any changes based on these observations?

  _____

  _____

  _____

  _____

  _____

Activity: _____

- What is my child's experience when participating in this activity, and how does that experience affect my child's brain?

  _____

  _____

  _____

  _____

  _____

- Is this activity producing "healthy" firing and wiring, or does my child seem to be developing some negative associations from the activity?

_____

_____

_____

_____

_____

- Do you want to make any changes based on these observations?

_____

_____

_____

_____

_____

We cannot, nor should we want to, protect our kids from all adversity and negative experiences. Challenging experiences are an important part of growing up, helping children develop resilience, acquire internal skills needed to cope with stress and failure, and learn to respond with flexibility. By helping kids make sense of their experiences, these challenges are more likely to be encoded as "learning experiences," rather than associations that limit them in the future.

BRAIN C #3 — THE BRAIN IS COMPLEX

The third Brain C (the brain's complexity) reminds us that when our kids are upset, or when they're acting in ways we don't like, we can appeal to different "parts" of their brains—to different regions and ways the brain functions, with different parental responses activating different circuitry. In other words, we can appeal to one part of the brain to get one result, and another part to get a different result.

We know that when our children are calm and in a receptive state of mind, they're capable of absorbing the lessons we're trying to teach. And when they're upset, their primitive brain takes control, shifting their focus to defending themselves from threat of attack. When they're in a reactive state like this, they can't learn.

Again: _The brain is either in a receptive state or a reactive state. Since the point of discipline is to teach, we can discipline effectively only when a child's brain is in a receptive state._

So how do we move our upset children from reactive to receptive? The first step is _recognizing_ that your child is upset _before_ you attempt to discipline his behavior.

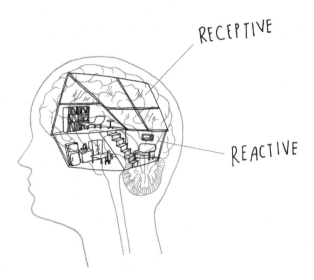

Reactive or Receptive?

How often do you think you try to discipline when your kids are reactive? It's probably more often than you realize. Most of us don't notice we're doing it until it's too late and we've already escalated a small upset into a big meltdown. Continuing to remind an overtired and hungry toddler that he needs to use his words when he's upset is a pretty sure sign you're disciplining into the black hole of reactivity.

But, the more aware you become of how your child behaves when he's at *the beginning stages of being upset*, the more you'll be able to discipline in a way that allows you to avoid the blowups and meltdowns while still teaching the coping skills and behaviors you want your child to learn.

Take a moment to think about the ways your child shows you his moods. When he's calm how does he speak to the people he's with? How does he hold his body? What sort of facial expressions does he make when he's relaxed and happy? What do you notice he does when he's feeling at ease? In the space below write down the details you notice when your child is in a calm, receptive state.

RECEPTIVE	
TONE OF VOICE	
BODY LANGUAGE	
FACIAL EXPRESSIONS	
ACTIONS	

Next, think about what your child is like when he's about to lose it—what is he like when he's furious, totally overwhelmed, or inconsolable? In the space below, write down all the details you've noticed about your child when he's at his most reactive and upset.

REACTIVE	
TONE OF VOICE	
BODY LANGUAGE	
FACIAL EXPRESSIONS	
ACTIONS	

When you notice your child showing any of these signs, it's a clue for you to tune in to what's going on in his world. When you discipline *proactively* like this, you'll notice that gentle correction or words of advice will often result in your child accepting help or altering his behavior with much less drama.

Are You Engaging or Enraging?

Sometimes we may find ourselves responding to our distressed child in a way that *amplifies* his distress, causing *more* reactivity. So now let's let you think about cause and effect when it comes to your child's behavior.

Begin by making a list, in the trigger column, of what sets your child off and makes her upset (losing at a board game, having an unexpected change of plans, feeling left out…). In the next column, name the corresponding reaction from you that would enrage your child's downstairs brain and upset her further? In other words, once your child is already upset, what's a typical reaction from you that would enrage your child? Then finally, move to the last column and name something you could do that would, instead, engage her upstairs brain and calm your child down. Don't judge yourself—we all have moments where we respond in less-than-helpful ways. The point here is to get clear about your own behaviors and what effect they have on your child, and whether your actions lead to reactivity or receptivity.

See below for an example and then continue to add your own.

CHILD'S TRIGGER	Having to turn off the TV before he's ready.
ENRAGE	When he starts crying, I say something like, "Sorry, but you've already had too much screen time today. Some kids don't get to watch TV at all."
ENGAGE	I let him express that he's upset, then empathize with him: "I know you want to keep watching. I can see you're sad because I'm turning off the TV. But we already watched the show, and now I've got something fun to show you."

CHILD'S TRIGGER	
ENRAGE	
ENGAGE	

CHILD'S TRIGGER	
ENRAGE	
ENGAGE	

CHILD'S TRIGGER	
ENRAGE	
ENGAGE	

It's clear from the list you just made that you know a number of ways to approach your child that don't feel like a threat, that engage his downstairs brain, and that help you get your point across effectively.

INSTEAD OF ENRAGING THE DOWNSTAIRS BRAIN...

ENGAGE THE UPSTAIRS BRAIN

Left-Brain Logic for Right-Brain Emotions

Still, even when we understand the importance of connecting to our child's emotions to help them calm down so they can be responsive instead of reactive, too often we rely on left-brain logic to deal with right-brain emotions.

Below you'll find three scenarios that commonly upset children. For each one, circle your most likely response in a similar circumstance.

It's time to leave the playground but your child refuses. When he starts to scream and cry you:

    a. Tell him you will give him a treat if he stops crying and comes with you.

    b. Remind him, as you pack up his toys, that he can't always get what he wants just because he cries. Even though his crying continues, you hold firm to leaving. After all, remaining consistent shows that you mean what you say.

    c. Acknowledge that he's upset and that you understand how hard it is to leave when he's having so much fun. Continue to empathize and give words to his feelings. Once he calms down enough, tell him you can be flexible this time so he can play for 5 more minutes and then it'll be time to go. You follow through with leaving after 5 minutes, even if it upsets him.

    d. Explain—in detail so he can understand the big picture—that it's almost time for lunch and you have to pick up his brother from day care by 2:00, so if you don't leave now you will be too rushed to make him the spaghetti he wanted to eat because it takes 20 minutes to get home from the park and you want to have enough time to do everything.

At her soccer game your child fails to block a goal that results in her team losing the game. She's angry with the other player for making her look stupid. She's angry with herself for letting her team down. She's a ball of nerves when you pick her up, lashing out at everyone. When she cries to you that she doesn't want to play soccer anymore you:

    a. Remind her of all the great games she's played, how much her teammates rely on her, and how she can practice more so next time she'll be sure to stop all the goals.

    b. Give her a big hug then offer to take her to that new movie she said she wanted to see if she stops crying about the game.

    c. Empathize with how awful it feels to let other people down, how embarrassing it is to make a mistake publically, how scary it is to try again after failing at something.

    d. Listen to her complain about the game for a while and then tell her that she can't keep crying about this forever; she needs to move on. Remind her that it's just a game and it's not such a big deal to lose once in a while.

You're playing with your child when his younger sibling tries to join in. As you agree, the older child refuses, pushing away the younger one. A battle over having time alone with you begins. You:

    a. Tell them you're tired of this old argument and that you don't want to be with either one of them until they figure out how to get along with each other.

    b. Tell them you have a new LEGO set that neither of them has seen yet and you'll build it with them if they can stop fighting.

c. Tell your little one to take a break where he has something to entertain himself for a few minutes so you can talk to your older one. When he's alone, and before you start talking, ask if he'd like a hug. Remind him that he's very important to you and that you love your time alone with him. When you feel him sink in and reconnect with you, gently ask what he thinks will happen if his little brother joins in.

d. Tell both kids be quiet and sit down because you are going to explain why it's so important for siblings to be friends with each other, how much it means to you that your kids are friends, and what life would be life if they never learn how to get along.

Look over your responses to this exercise. If you answered anything other than "c" for any of the scenarios, it's likely you've had times where you shift into autopilot and react with left-brain logic, or other brain-enraging tactics, when your child really needs a more emotionally attuned, right-brain response. What steps would you need to take to become more aware, in the moment, of what response your child really needs? Write your thoughts here.

_____

_____

_____

_____

No-Drama Discipline Builds The Brain

You've seen how the Whole-Brain approach makes your life easier and less stressful because it allows you to diffuse potentially explosive situations with your kids. You also know that it helps you communicate how much you love your children while setting boundaries that keep them safe. But, beyond that, No-Drama Discipline actually strengthens neural connections between upstairs and downstairs parts of the brain, and these connections lead to personal insight, responsibility, flexible decision-making, empathy, and morality.

In other words, the way we interact with our kids when they're upset significantly affects how their brains develop, and therefore what kind of people they are, both today and in the years to come.

Keep in mind that every time you discipline, you can use that moment as an opportunity to practice building important skills and help wire those experiences into your child's brain.

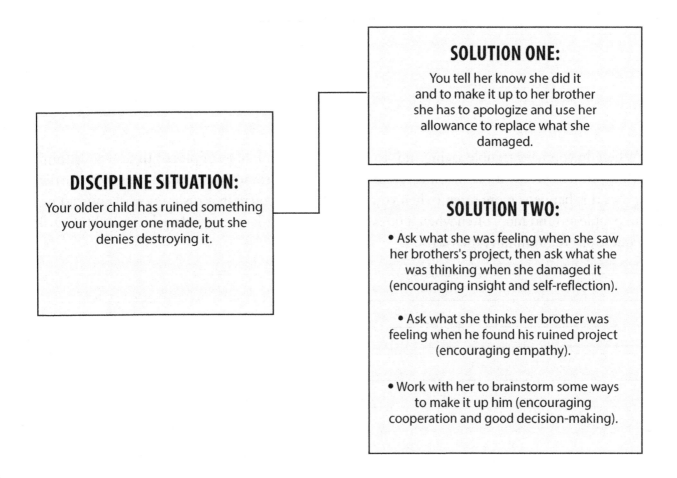

It's like that old adage, "Give a man a fish and he'll eat for a day. Teach a man to fish and he'll eat for a lifetime." When we solve our children's problems for them, we're focused only on the short-term goal of ending the conflict in the moment. The more we help our kids make positive and productive choices on their own, the more they build these skills for themselves and the less discipline will ultimately be necessary.

BUILDING THE BRAIN BY SETTING LIMITS

One of the best ways we help build our child's brain is by setting limits. Take time now to reflect on how you interact with your child when you set limits. Do you let her experience the healthy guilt that allows her conscience to develop? Do you go beyond just good/bad and right/wrong, so that she actually thinks about her choices, and morality and ethics get wired into her brain?

How do you show your child which behaviors are acceptable and which aren't? Just write about the way you set limits.

_____

_____

_____

_____

_____

_____

When do you have trouble saying "no" to your child? Think of examples of times you let him do something either because it makes things easier on you, or for some other reason. Are there particular times that this happens more often (when you're tired, when you're in a rush, on weekends…) or are certain people around more often when it does happen (your in-laws, a privileged friend…)? Consider these questions for a minute, then write:

_____

_____

_____

_____

_____

_____

INSTEAD OF AN OUTRIGHT NO...

TRY A YES WITH A CONDITION

You might be surprised by how often you set and hold limits over the course of a day. In fact, we do it so often it's easy to miss numerous opportunities for teaching our children. For instance, many of us have experienced times when we've missed the opportunity to help our kids get comfortable with (or at least used to) the reality that they don't always get their way. In saying "yes" to avoid dealing with what comes along with our children not getting their way, we are side-stepping the fact that our kids need us to set limits so they learn how to set them for themselves.

On the other hand, maybe you're saying "no" more than you have to. Are there times you should give in more, or has "no" simply become your default response? Do you find yourself so concerned with not caving in to your child's whims that you've unwittingly become rigid?

Over the next few days, take the time to write down samples of when your kids ask you for things. As the requests happen, be mindful of the motivation behind each "yes" or "no" you give. Is it simply a knee-jerk response? Are you catching a moment to teach your child and wire new connections? Are your limits set with love and empathy, or coupled with anger and negative comments? Fill in the chart below with your observations.

CHILD'S REQUEST	MY RESPONSE

Now that you've made a visual representation of your limit setting habits, is there anything you'd like to improve upon or change? What steps do you need to take to make that happen? What support would you need to keep those changes in place? Write out your thoughts in the space below:

_____

_____

_____

_____

MISBEHAVIOR IS ACTUALLY A PLEA FOR HELP WITH SKILL-BUILDING

Every time our children misbehave, they give us an opportunity to understand them better, and get a better sense of what they need help learning. For many parents this is a radically different way of looking at behavior. Many of us grew up learning that a child having a meltdown in the grocery store is simply out of control and in need of punishment and consequences. But another way to view that same child is to see her as someone in need of help building her frustration tolerance. Behavior is communication about what skills still need to be built.

Let's let you apply that to your own kids. Look at the illustration below and then replace the little girl in the picture with your own child. Imagine your child doing something you don't like, then "reframe" your child's action in a way that acknowledges that she's simply lacking in certain skills, and needs your help to build them.

WHAT A PARENT SEES:

WHAT THE CHILD IS REALLY SAYING:

Using the set of boxes below, draw your own illustration of your child. Don't worry about your artistic skills—stick figures are just fine. All that matters is that you know what the drawing represents.

In the left-hand section, draw a picture of your child doing something you would normally discipline him for (teasing his sister, talking back to you, etc.). Then, on the right side, draw your child with a talk bubble like in our illustration. He might be saying, "I need to build skills waiting my turn," or "I need skill building when it comes to handling myself well and communicating my disappointment respectfully when I don't get my way." Do the same—focusing on a different behavior—in the second set of boxes.

Look at your drawings. Take in what your child has been trying to tell you through her behavior. Would your responses to her be different if she were able to describe her thoughts and feelings instead of acting them out? The answer is probably yes. Similar to the "Can't vs. Won't" idea, this shift in perspective can be a game changer for many people. It's much harder to respond with anger to a child asking for help.

However, your child still has so much brain development left to happen, and so many skills to master, for now it's unlikely she'll be able to make things that easy for you. But when you realize that these "misbehavior moments" aren't just miserable experiences to endure, but actually are opportunities for knowledge and growth, you can reframe the whole experience and recognize it as a chance to build the brain and create something meaningful and significant in your child's life.

THREE REFLECTIONS

Before we close this chapter, we want to offer three reflections where we ask questions to help you think about your approach to discipline with your kids.

REFLECTION #1 — HOW PATIENT CAN YOU BE?

Of course you know that you can't program your kids to obey your expectations and rules as if they were robots. But, at times you may forget that being human means your kids come with their own emotions, desires, and agendas—and that means your children aren't always going to go along with what you want them to do. Think about that right now. Can you handle that reality? Process it for a minute within yourself.

Can you accept the fact that your kids will continue to mess up, and things will stay messy sometimes, no matter how hard you try or how hard you discipline? What makes that difficult for you? What will you need to remind yourself that this approach is working over the long term, even though there may not be the magical instant solution you crave? Write your thoughts about this process and answer those questions in the space below:

_____

_____

_____

_____

_____

_____

_____

_____

REFLECTION #2 — HOW WILLING ARE YOU TO EXPRESS LOVE TO YOUR KIDS, EVEN AS YOU DISCIPLINE THEM?

Even when discipline doesn't work out perfectly, it gives you a chance to communicate to your kids how much you love and respect them, no matter what. No matter how far off track your discipline plan has gone, No-Drama discipline allows you to communicate to your children, *"I'm with you. I've got your back. Even when you're at your worst and I don't like the way you're acting, I love you, and I'm here for you. I understand you're having a hard time. And I am here."*

Does it seem possible to be simultaneously telling your children that you want them to change their behavior, while also letting them know you support them? Some may feel the two actions would be mutually exclusive, but it's important to note that this approach *doesn't* mean that you don't draw clear boundaries or observe family rules; rather, you're simply making sure that you communicate love as you do so.

Think now about an issue that seems to come up regularly between you and your child –a problem that you're having trouble getting on top of. The next time it happens, even if you don't like the way your child has acted, how can you communicate to them that you've got their back and love them despite everything? Write your thoughts in the space provided here:

_____

_____

_____

_____

REFLECTION #3 — CAN YOU LET GO OF YOUR DESIRE FOR PERFECTION AS A PARENT?

The truth is, you're going to mess up—even after you read *No-Drama Discipline* and do all the exercises in this workbook. And even though we're considered experts on parenting, we continue to mess up as well. We're human. And so are you. The thing is, being a perfect parent isn't the goal you should be striving for. Can you imagine how hard it would be on your kids to have a parent who did everything perfectly? How would they learn to accept their own imperfections, to take responsibility for their mistakes, to repair a bond they share with someone they care about?

Of course you want to do your best for your kids, but it's important to remember that even your mistakes as a parent can be extremely valuable for your children. You're more likely to reach your parenting goals by working toward increasing your awareness of, and insight into, your own thoughts and behaviors, than you ever will by focusing on being an ideal parent—and feeling guilty that you're not.

This self-awareness is an essential step in becoming the sort of parent who responds intuitively when your child behaves in a way you don't like. Letting go of the judgments and negative beliefs you have about *your own* past reactions and behavior allows you to see not only the value in the existence of those actions, but also the best way to move forward with your children. And in order to let go, you might even need to do some forgiving.

A Reflection on Self-Forgiveness

Find a quiet place to sit where you'll be free from distraction for a while. Close your eyes and clear your mind with a few deep breaths—breathing in through your nose for a count of 5, holding your breath for a count of 5, and then breathing out through your mouth for another count of 5. Repeat this sequence three times - or until you feel your body soften and your mind calmly settle. Begin this exercise by listing all of your good qualities as a parent (*I'm playful, I'm a good listener, I make the best macaroni and cheese...*). Write it all down so you have a record of it all. You can do that here:

_____

_____

_____

_____

Keeping in mind everything you know that makes you a good parent, call up to your memory a recent interaction with your child that you feel guilty about. Picture in your mind's eye your child's face and posture in the moment of conflict. How did he look? Remember how you spoke, the tone and the words you used. Bring into consciousness everything that happened—especially the parts that seem most difficult to face. It's those details that hold the key to what is keeping you stuck in a sense of guilt, embarrassment, or shame.

Close your eyes and take note of how your body feels as you hold this memory. Scan yourself with your mind's eye from head to toe and notice where you feel tension or restrictions. Do you feel anything more strongly in one part of your body or another? Are there any words or visuals that pop up for you? Write down whatever comes to your mind as you do this:

_____

_____

_____

_____

Next, as you sort through the details of the unpleasant interaction with your child, think about each step you feel guilty about. Did you lose control? Did you make him cry? Did she look scared? Did you yell? Maybe you said something unkind, or slammed a door. Maybe you ignored him, or rolled your eyes when she complained.

Whatever you did, the next step is to acknowledge each of these actions by taking responsibility for it. You can write it down in the space below.

I am responsible for (*mocking him, losing my patience…*).

I am responsible for _____

I am responsible for _____

I am responsible for _____

As you look at your list, remind yourself that taking responsibility means that it's your job to repair with your child and to take steps toward making better choices in the future. That's it. The guilt that you've been holding on to has no place anymore. You're allowed to release it. Repeat to yourself:

I am a good parent.

I forgive myself for what I did poorly in the past.

I forgive myself for what I didn't know.

I forgive myself for being a work in progress.

I am working on knowing better so I can do better.

I am a good parent.

Take a deep breath in and let it out slowly.

Next, get specific about your self-forgiveness by taking responsibility for your actions. Acknowledge to yourself what you've done to learn from this experience *(I can tell that when I don't eat all day I am much more likely to lose my temper...)* and what you've done to repair the situation *(I explained that my hunger made me extra grumpy...)*. Write down anything else you need to learn or do to put this situation behind you:

_____

_____

_____

_____

_____

_____

Repeat to yourself:

I am a good parent.

I forgive myself for what I did poorly in the past.

I forgive myself for what I didn't know.

I forgive myself for being a work in progress.

I am working on knowing better so I can do better.

I am a good parent.

Take a deep breath in and let it out slowly.

Now, think once more about that unpleasant interaction you had with your child and bring your awareness back to your body. What do you notice now? Do you feel the same heaviness, or is there a sense of relief? That relief comes from acknowledging your own responsibility, repairing with your child, forgiving yourself, then moving on.

CHAPTER 3

From Tantrum to Tranquility: Connection Is the Key

When we offer comfort when our kids are upset, when we listen to their feelings, when we communicate how much we love them even when they've messed up: when we respond in these ways, we significantly impact the way their brains develop and the kind of people they'll be, both now and as they move into adolescence and adulthood.

— No-Drama Discipline

Most of us find that it's generally easy to be supportive and in tune with our children when they're happy and behaving in a way we like. It can be quite a bit harder to respond the same way when they're upset, grumpy, or throwing a tantrum. But those moments of distress are actually when our kids most need us to maintain that emotional connection. In doing so, we create an opportunity for learning, and we model for our children that there are calmer, more loving ways to interact when you're upset with someone.

CONNECT BEFORE YOU REDIRECT

We began Chapter 3 of *No-Drama Discipline* with a story about Michael, Matthias, and the Lego Massacre. Take a few minutes to review that story now. You'll notice that we explained the many ways Michael's connect-first approach was effective in that situation.

Think now about discipline moments with your children. Ask yourself, "What's my typical initial response when I don't like something my kids have done?" To what extent would you say you tend to connect before you redirect, reprimand, or correct your kids? Using the following chart, circle the answer that fits best.

How often do you connect first, before redirecting?

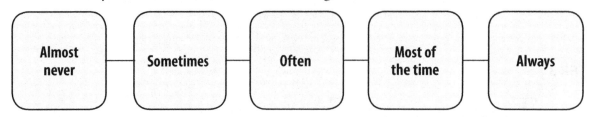

| Almost never | Sometimes | Often | Most of the time | Always |

Now, take a few minutes to write your thoughts about this question. Why do you think you respond with redirection first as frequently (or infrequently) as you do? Are there times when it's more (or less) likely to happen? What do you notice about the times when you connect *before* you redirect? Does it depend on how you feel? How big the infraction is? Something else? Write here:

_____

_____

_____

_____

As you think about these discipline interactions with your child, and any patterns (repeated behaviors, settings, actions…) that tend to make you respond one way or another what do you notice? What would you need in your life to be able to increase your ability to use a connect-first approach with your children *(time each day for yourself, more "fun time" spent with your child, less stress at work…)*? Use the space below for your answers.

_____

_____

_____

_____

PROACTIVE PARENTING

While connecting first is the most effective way to approach discipline once your child's behavior gets out of hand, proactive parenting decreases your need to use discipline methods in the first place. When we parent proactively, we watch for times we can tell that misbehavior and/or a meltdown is in our children's future—it's just over the horizon of where we are now—and we step in and try to guide them around the potential landmine. So, when you see your child's behavior trending in a direction you don't like, if you **HALT** to ask yourself if she is **h**ungry, **a**ngry, **l**onely, or **t**ired, you're more likely to get ahead of that situation before it escalates, thus reducing the need to take any sort of disciplinary action.

INSTEAD OF PARENTING REACTIVELY...

PARENT PROACTIVELY

In every family there are bound to be a number of discipline situations that parents face on a regular basis with their children. Maybe your child falls apart whenever he's losing a competitive game. Maybe he can't keep his feelings in check each time his sister gets attention. Perhaps homework is a struggle every night, or you constantly butt heads over getting chores done. Whatever the specifics are, if it's happening frequently enough that it feels like a familiar battle, you've got an opportunity to parent proactively and get in front of any impending behavior meltdowns.

In the space that follows, list your family's typical discipline scenarios. Then, after each one, take a few minutes to write down at least one thing you can do proactively that could lessen the need to discipline your child.

Typical Behavior:

_____

Proactive Parenting Action:

_____

_____

_____

_____

_____

Typical Behavior:

_____

Proactive Parenting Action:

_____

_____

_____

_____

_____

Typical Behavior:

_____

Proactive Parenting Action:

_____

_____

_____

_____

_____

Now that you've given proactive parenting some thought in relation to your own family, let's help you make a cheat sheet for yourself of the ideas you came up with. How it looks doesn't matter—just know that you're going to keep it somewhere visible to remind yourself of your proactive parenting intentions. Here's an example of one using the HALT reminder:

HUNGRY?	• Have healthy snacks available throughout the play date. • Have protein snack ready after school so he has energy to do his homework. • Reduce his sugar intake, especially on days when he has to focus for long periods.
ANGRY?	• Get him to move his body—challenge him to a Wii sports match! • Set up a suggestion box in the kitchen where anyone can express ideas, frustrations, requests etc. Discuss anything received at weekly family meetings. • Create a feelings chart to help him verbalize his emotions.
LONELY?	• Ask if he wants his scheduled 15 minutes of "special time" alone with you right now instead of when it was planned for. • Make a show of putting away your phone/computer/work and let him know that he's what's most important right now. • Ask if you can join in doing whatever he's doing.
TIRED?	• Suggest a quiet activity, like watching a movie, so the family can be together but he doesn't have the focus directly on him. • Change of scenery. Get outside! A few minutes of fresh air, nature, and bare feet on grass can help shift a mood. • Set up frequent breaks during homework hours to get the energy flowing—stretch/move the body/dance.

Proactive parenting isn't always easy—it can take a good deal of effort and awareness on your part. But the more you watch for the signs that your child is heading toward a rough patch, and the more often you're able to step in with help or distraction, the less time you'll spend cleaning up the aftermath of meltdowns and blow ups.

WHY CONNECT FIRST?

As much as being proactive will mean less time spent disciplining, it's not possible to anticipate or avoid everything. There are going to be times that unwanted or reactive behavior just happens. And when it does, we need to fight the urge to immediately punish, lecture, lay down the law, distract, minimize, or even positively redirect right away. Instead, we need to connect.

As we explain in *No-Drama Discipline*, three basic benefits appear when we connect first. Let's give you a chance to apply these ideas to your own situation with your child.

BENEFIT #1 — CONNECTION MOVES A CHILD FROM REACTIVITY TO RECEPTIVITY

Remember, it's when our kids are most upset that they need us the most. The first thing they need from us is to help them calm down. When we connect with our children they can begin to regain control and allow their upstairs brain to engage again—moving them into a state where they can be receptive to what we want to teach them.

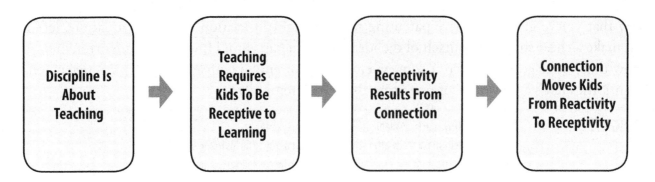

Connection offers the sense of "feeling felt," and it's a need for everyone—adults and children alike. Think back, for a moment, to the last time you felt really sad or angry or upset. Now imagine that the person you love and trust most responded to you by saying something like, "You need to calm down," or "It's not *that* big of a deal." Imagine you were told to "go be by yourself until you're calm and ready to be nice and happy." How would you feel if you didn't get the connection you craved when you're upset? Would you want to take advice or suggestions from the person who denied you that connection? Would you feel more upset or would you be able to calm down and listen? Take a few minutes to picture this scenario and then write your thoughts in the space below:

_____

_____

_____

_____

CONNECTION MOVES A CHILD FROM REACTIVITY TO RECEPTIVITY

Now, consider what you've written about yourself and apply it to your child. Think back to a recent interaction where you weren't able to connect with her before jumping in to correct or lecture. Can you see the scene from her point of view more easily now? Are any of her reactions similar to yours? Was she receptive to your advice, or did she continue to be reactive? In contrast, recall a moment where you *did* connect first—what differences do you notice? Write your thoughts here:

What connection does, essentially, is integrate the brain and make it possible for our children to regain control of their emotions and bodies. Because connection helps the different parts of the brain begin working together as a coordinated whole, it's not surprising that our kids can then make more thoughtful choices and handle themselves better.

BENEFIT #2 — CONNECTION BUILDS THE BRAIN

As we explain in *No-Drama Discipline*, "When we offer comfort when our kids are upset; when we listen to their feelings; when we communicate how much we love them even when they've messed up: when we respond in these ways, we significantly impact the way their brains develop and the kind of people they'll be, both now and as they move into adolescence and adulthood."

Take a minute now and read that sentence again, paying close attention to how you feel as you read those words. Do you feel affirmed in terms of how you typically interact with your child? Does it make you want to do things differently? What sort of support would you need in your life to make those changes? Share your thoughts and feelings in the space below:

In addition to helping your children know that you love them even at their worst, connection is about making your kids feel understood, valued, and accepted at all times. Moments as simple as reading a book together or asking your child's advice on what tie to wear that day, when done regularly—and with intention—can make a significant change in the relationship you have with your child.

WHAT CONNECTION LOOKS LIKE:

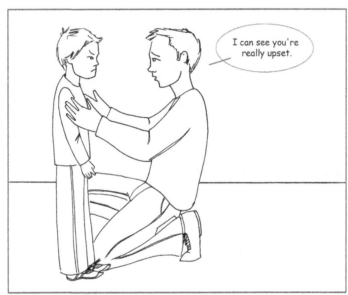

Begin making a list with as many ways to connect with your child as you can think of. Your list can include any type of moments, like not taking calls when you're with your kids, asking to play a video game with your child, sharing a back and forth journal where you ask questions of each other, or whatever. Create your list in the space below. Use an additional sheet of paper if needed.

1. _____

2. _____

3. _____

4. _____

5. _____

6. _____

7. _____

Now that you have all of these great ideas fresh in your mind, for the next few days make it a point to find moments throughout the day to connect with your child.

- Make note, as best you can, of how his physical and emotional states shift when you do connect *(does he hold his body in a more relaxed way, is he smiling more, is his tone of voice more gentle…).*
- Be aware of whether your child's behavior changes over the period of time you're tracking, and make note what those changes look like *(is he treating others any differently, is he more agreeable/ more flexible, is he less prone to argue or disagree…).*
- When you're finished with this exercise, ask yourself what, if anything, has changed about your relationship with your child *(do you feel as though you know him better, do you feel closer to each other, is there less tension between you…).*

Write your observations throughout this exercise in the section below. We've divided it into three days, but feel free to make notes for as many days as you wish.

DAY 1:

_____

_____

_____

_____

_____

_____

DAY 2:

_____

_____

_____

_____

DAY 3:

_____

_____

_____

_____

An integrated, connected, relationship with your child literally changes her brain. These small moments of attunement strengthen the connection between different areas of the brain, helping create the executive functions of self-regulation—balanced emotions, focused attention, impulse control, and empathy—that are key to reducing dramatic and unwanted behavior in your family.

BENEFIT #3 — CONNECTION DEEPENS YOUR RELATIONSHIP WITH YOUR CHILD

Moments of conflict can make it really hard to respond with loving guidance instead of exasperation, irritation, and anger. In fact, connecting in those moments might be the last thing you want to do. However, how you respond when you're not happy with your kids' behavior can be among the most important opportunities you have to impact the development of your relationship and your child's sense of self.

CONNECTION DEEPENS YOUR RELATIONSHIP WITH YOUR CHILD

Take a look at how this plays out in your own family. Begin by filling in each box on the left side of the chart below with a discipline challenge you sometimes face with your child. We'll have you fill in the rest of the chart in a minute. Right now, just list one discipline challenge in each of the "challenging behavior" boxes.

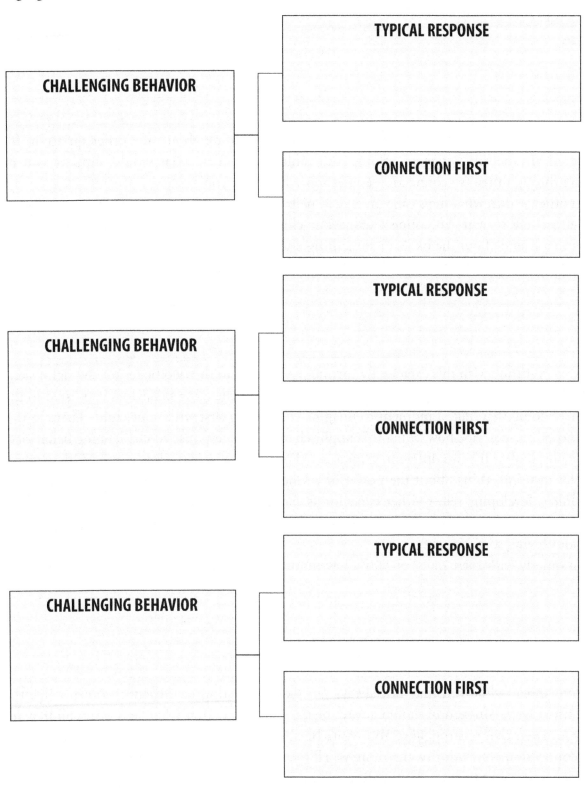

Now look at these three examples. Are any of the behaviors more triggering for you than others? If so, why do you think that is? Are you unnerved by loud noises? Does being ignored by your child remind you of feeling that way when you were younger? Does chaos make you feel out-of-control? Take a minute to write out your thoughts about what might be triggering upset feelings within you in these disciplinary encounters.

_____

_____

_____

Before we move on to the other boxes in the chart, think about one other question: If you've discovered any personal triggers among your child's behaviors, what would support you most in working through them so connection comes more freely for you?

In other words, what steps can you take to help you deal with your personal feelings of frustration more effectively so you can connect with your child more fully? Maybe it's getting more sleep, or talking to a friend about the issue, or something else. Write about it here.

_____

_____

_____

Now continue with this exercise by turning your focus to the two boxes on the right side. Fill in the top boxes with how you *typically* react to each of the challenging behaviors you listed to the left.

After doing that, take a moment to imagine connecting first with your child. Then, in the lower left-hand boxes, describe how doing this might change your response to challenging behaviors.

Finally, look at the two different responses—the upper one and the lower one. With these practical examples in mind, think about the power of connection. Consider what impact connection has on your child's developing self. On her behavior as she grows up. How might a connected relationship with her parents change the way she relates to others? What could she be learning about being loved and about loving someone else?

Sit quietly with these questions for a few minutes, then write.

_____

_____

_____

Remember, while you may not always *feel* like connecting in difficult moments like the ones you've listed here, connection should always be the goal. No matter what ages your children are, they need you when they're struggling. You won't be able to connect first every time, but the more you make connection your priority, the more you'll fortify your relationship and the more your kids will know they can count on you. Best of all, you'll be teaching by role modeling, guiding by what you do and not only by what you say.

WHAT ABOUT TANTRUMS? AREN'T WE SUPPOSED TO IGNORE THEM?

When your child has lost control of his body and/or emotions and is having a tantrum, it's important to remember that it's a sign that the different parts of his brain aren't working together as a coordinated whole. If he could, he'd tell you that his downstairs brain has hijacked his upstairs brain and that he doesn't have the capacity to be flexible or manage his feelings at the moment. And he'd probably also tell you that right now what he needs is some empathy, support, and help calming down. Of course, he can't actually verbalize all of that. But even if he isn't using words to say it, *your child is always communicating with you through his behavior.*

Let's back up for a moment and take a look at how *you* feel when your child throws a tantrum. What emotions come up for you *(irritation, resentment, anger…)*? What fears do you have *(he's never going to learn, she'll always be doing this, he'll never make any friends if he keeps behaving this way…)*? What, if anything, do you notice about your body when you know you have to respond to a tantrum *(slumped posture, clenched jaw, tight stomach…)*? Use the space below for your answers.

_____

_____

_____

_____

Our reactions to out-of-control behavior in our children are often influenced by beliefs shaped in our own childhood about what's acceptable behavior and what isn't. As adults we don't have to simply accept every thought we have as the truth—we have the ability to look closely and question the beliefs we hold.

How were your own out-of-control moments handled when you were a child *(yelling, time outs, anger…)*? What do you think those experiences taught you about acceptable behavior *(children should be seen and not heard, I'm loveable only when I'm good, it's not safe to say no…)*? And last, how do you think your experiences as a child affect the way you respond to tantrums with your own children? Take a few moments to consider these questions and then write your answers in the space provided:

_____

_____

_____

_____

Understanding your feelings about your child's out-of-control behavior ultimately helps you to be emotionally responsive and attuned to her more often. Responding that way on a regular basis builds your child's ability to self-regulate and self-soothe over time, leading to more independence and resiliency – and less tantrums.

This sort of connection can take practice, since many parents are accustomed to viewing unwanted behavior strictly as an unpleasant experience they need to get through or to stop as soon as possible at all costs.

Instead, we'd like you to challenge you to reframe the way you think about tantrums. All behavior is communication. So do you know what your child is actually telling you when he's upset and out of control? Take a look at the tantrum scenarios described below, and the examples of what a child might be trying to communicate through her behavior.

TANTRUM BEHAVIOR	WHAT'S ACTUALLY BEING COMMUNICATED:
Extreme irritation and continued complaining about unexpectedly having to go along with her sibling to an afterschool appointment.	I need help managing my anxiety over changes in plans I wasn't expecting.
Anger about being pushed to do "stupid" homework that's "too HARD" and has "no purpose."	I need help knowing that I'm OK even when I'm not good at things.
Sour face, defensive body language, refusing every alternative option suggested.	I need help with being flexible when things don't go my way.

Now, try the same exercise using descriptions of tantrums your own child has had. Write all the details you remember about her behavior in the column on the left. Next, read over what you wrote as if you were an outside observer—one without a personal reaction to the behavior. Then in the column to the right, make a guess about what your child was *really* trying to express with that tantrum.

TANTRUM BEHAVIOR	WHAT I'M ACTUALLY SAYING IS…

Because out-of-control behavior is one way for children to tell us that they need help, we're left with a choice in terms of what message we send them when they act in ways we don't like. We're sure you wouldn't actually tell your child, "Mom and Dad only want to be around you when you're happy and well-behaved," or, "You have to figure out your big emotions by yourself without our help." But that's often the message we're sending our kids when we react to their behavior without empathy and emotional connection.

The following illustration offers two different messages a parent can send when responding to a tantrum. On the page after that, you'll see some examples of different parental responses to tantrums. After reading through them, decide which ones are examples of disconnecting messages like #1, and which are examples of connecting messages like #2.

MESSAGE 1:

MESSAGE 2:

1. "Are you still upset about that? You really need to get over it already. When you're ready to stop whining about it, let me know. I'll be downstairs—maybe we can go do something together when you're in a better mood."

    Connecting or disconnecting? _____

2. "If you keep speaking to me in that tone of voice, I'm done talking to you. What do you have to be so angry about anyway? It's not like you have real problems. When you're in this mood it's really hard to be around you!"

    Connecting or disconnecting? _____

3. "Wow. That's a pretty huge reaction for you. I won't let you hurt my body, so I'm going to hold these blocks you were throwing. But come sit in my lap. Tell me what's going on."

    Connecting or disconnecting? _____

Although you want your child's tantrums to end as quickly as possible, that shouldn't be your main focus. In fact, the larger goal of connecting gets you there a whole lot faster in the short run, and achieves a whole lot more in the long run. By providing empathy, your calm presence, and by focusing on what your child is communicating through his behavior instead of focusing on the behavior itself, you're building your child's capacity to handle himself better in the future – ultimately, reducing the need for disciplining your child.

How Do You Connect Without Spoiling a Child?

Although many parents worry that a connect-first approach will result in spoiled children and reinforcing their unwanted behaviors, it's important to understand that giving kids love and attention *isn't* spoiling them. What *is* spoiling them, however, is when we give them everything they want, when we rarely set a boundary because we don't want them to be unhappy, or when we rescue our kids from dealing with or feeling anything difficult, rather than just being with them as they walk through hard times.

Take time now to think about times you may have made life too easy for your own child *(going to a teacher about a low grade instead of letting your child speak up himself, not giving your child chores or responsibilities at home…)*. What do you think your child believes about himself because of these experiences *(I don't have to work hard in school—my teachers always change my grades when my parents tell them to, I'm not responsible enough to be trusted—so I don't have to help out…)*? Do any of your child's resulting beliefs sound like those of a spoiled child? Write about your observations.

_____

_____

_____

_____

In contrast, recall moments where you *resisted* the urge to solve your child's problems, instead helping her figure out solutions on her own while supporting her through the discomfort and struggle.

Why do you think you were able to hold yourself back this time, but not other times? How did these moments differ from when you fixed her problems for her? What did your child learn about herself from these interactions?

_____

_____

_____

_____

We're all in agreement that overindulgence is unhelpful for children, unhelpful for parents, and unhelpful for the relationship. But connection *isn't* about spoiling children, coddling them, or inhibiting their independence. Nor is it about rescuing kids from adversity. Connection is about walking through the hard times with our children and being there for them when they're emotionally suffering, just like we would be if they were physically suffering. And remember, when we do this, we're building their resilience and independence!

YOU CAN CONNECT WHILE STILL SETTING LIMITS

When we talk about connecting with a child who's struggling to control herself, we don't mean you allow her to behave however she wants.

SET LOVING LIMITS

Children need limits in order to feel safe and secure—to know what's expected of them in a given environment. But children do need to know that we care about what they're going through—so when boundaries are set it needs to be done with firm, *but loving*, guidance.

However, the knee-jerk reaction many parents have to the need for limit setting is, instead, a command-and-demand approach to discipline. Take a look at the examples below. Do any of the reactions sound familiar (if not from you, then from people you know)?

UNWANTED BEHAVIOR	COMMAND AND DEMAND
Siblings fighting over a coloring book and crayons. The older one won't let her sister use it.	"Share with your sister, or neither of you can use it!"
Your child is grumpy and flops on the couch complaining about how bored he is. The longer it goes on, the more discontented he gets.	"Stop whining and use your regular voice."
Your child is impulsive and impatient about claiming his prize at the end of a class.	"Stop grabbing and wait your turn!"

INSTEAD OF COMMANDING AND DEMANDING...

CONNECT WHILE SETTING LIMITS

Although extinguishing unwanted behavior as soon as possible is the intention most parents have when they approach discipline by commanding and demanding, it often leaves kids defensive and more oppositional than before. Without connection first, not only is your child's brain too dysregulated to take in what you want her to understand about limits and acceptable behavior, but you're also giving her orders without showing some understanding of how she feels about the situation—it's the perfect set up for an epic power struggle.

In contrast, connecting with your child when you step in to set limits is a win-win situation. Among other things:

✓ You reduce the possibility that you'll lose your cool because connection also integrates *your* brain.
✓ You model the type of behavior you want her to develop.
✓ You deepen your relationship with your child.
✓ You wire your child's brain to expect that her needs will be met and that she's unconditionally loved. That way, even when she encounters difficulties with people in life, she can operate from a position of knowing that she's lovable, even when she's not loved by everyone.

As a final exercise, think about how connection while setting limits might look in your family. In the chart below, fill in the left-hand column with examples of behaviors that call for discipline in your household. In the column on the right, list examples of how to respond to those behaviors in ways that allow you to stay connected, instead of blaming and shaming your child.

UNWANTED BEHAVIOR	CONNECTION WHILE SETTING LIMITS

We want our children to know that they're seen, heard, and loved by their parents—even when they do something wrong. When we show that we value and respect a child's inner world, while also holding him to standards about his behavior, he feels secure and is able to thrive. It's from that place of being truly known and loved that children can fully develop their resiliency, resourcefulness, and relational skills.

CHAPTER 4

No-Drama Connection in Action

*If we focus only on our child's behavior (her external world) and neglect the reasons
behind that behavior (her internal world), then we'll concentrate only on the
symptoms, not the cause that's producing them. And if we consider only the symptoms,
we'll have to keep treating those symptoms over and over again.*

— *No-Drama Discipline*

As you begin to practice a connection-first approach to discipline, it's important to remember that there's no magical, one-size-fits-all strategy for putting an end to unwanted behavior. Responding to every behavior and every child in the same way and with the same intensity not only makes little sense, but it also removes the opportunity to attune to your children when they need you most. On the other hand, response flexibility—responding to behavior only *after* considering both the state of mind of your individual child and the specific situation at hand—leads you and your child toward connection and, ultimately, less drama.

In chapter 3 you got clear about how often you fall back on one-size-fits-all strategies to handle behavior challenges. Take a minute now to look back at your answers before we move on to **No-Drama Connection Principles.**

CONNECTION PRINCIPLE #1 — TURN DOWN THE SHARK MUSIC

You'll remember the shark music explanation from *No-Drama Discipline.* We all have moments when the chaos in our heads, or the fear-inducing music in the background, keeps us from being in the moment. "Shark music" keeps us trapped in our fears about the future, or stuck on what's happened in the past, making us reactive and unable to focus on what our children really need in this moment, or what they're actually communicating.

The way we perceive a situation is entirely dependent on how we experience it. In other words, if you approach a discipline situation with your head full of everything that could go wrong (or has already gone wrong) you're going to react like someone defending herself from a threat. However, if you were to experience the exact same behavior with a sense of calm and serenity, you're much more likely to respond in a peaceful way.

INSTEAD OF HEARING SHARK MUSIC...

CONNECT WITH YOUR CHILD WHO NEEDS YOU

The best way to fully understand this difference in perception is to experience firsthand the effects of shark music. To begin, choose two pieces of music. The first should be something that you find personally soothing, relaxing, and peaceful. Any calm piece of classical music should do. Then, choose a second piece that's something akin to the *Jaws* theme music: dark and threatening. If you Google "scary music," you'll easily find some good examples.

Next, set up your computer, or phone, to play a slideshow of your photos (past vacations, birthday parties, your children playing together…). Play the pictures through once with the peaceful music playing as background music. Notice how your body feels as you watch. Pay attention to the thoughts you have as you watch the slideshow and jot down notes in the space here:

_____

_____

_____

_____

Next, play the slideshow again, but this time set the menacing soundtrack you've chosen as the background music. Again, taking notes in the space below, pay careful attention to how your body reacts and what thoughts and feelings you have while watching the photos this time around.

_____

_____

_____

_____

Now, look over what you've written above and take notice of what changed for you as the music changed. Even though you were watching the same slideshow both times, how were your reactions different? How was your perception altered?

_____

_____

_____

_____

_____

As you think about how "shark music" can alter your perception, you may realize that most of the time you're only vaguely aware of the thoughts that run through your head each day—whether they're positive or negative. Yet, because this background noise affects everything from your body language and tone of voice, to how easily you maintain connection with your child, it's worthwhile to examine your theme song more deeply.

Now let's apply this exercise to your actual experiences with your kids. During challenging moments with your children, what would you list as your personal shark music? It might include fears about the future (*she's going to end up just like her brother; he's never going to learn this; how will I ever deal with her when she's a teenager if she's like this now...*) and/or your own internal dialogue crowding out your ability to be in the moment (*work distractions, resentments, frustrations...*). Write out your list below. What's your personal shark music?

_____

_____

_____

_____

_____

So if that's your shark music, what can you do about it? What, in other words, can you do to bring yourself back to the present moment and deal with the actual situation in front of you? Take the time now to list three ideas that could work best for you (*deep breathing, listing three things you love about your child, verbalizing your own feelings...*). This will be your personalized version of switching out that dark, menacing theme song for a peaceful and soothing soundtrack. You may need to try different strategies until you find a few that work for you, but having a few at your fingertips will greatly improve your ability to respond intentionally when your child is having a hard time.

1. _____

2. _____

3. _____

Once you're able to recognize the shark music playing in your head, you can shift your state of mind and stop parenting based on fear and past experiences that don't apply to the current scenario you face. And when you can do that, you'll find that response flexibility is a more attainable goal.

CONNECTION PRINCIPLE #2 — CHASE THE WHY

One of the worst byproducts of shark music is the parental tendency to make assumptions about our kids' motivations, rather than seeing what's actually going on in the moment. We often immediately blame and criticize, rather than being curious and chasing the why.

INSTEAD OF BLAMING AND CRITCIZING...

CHASE THE WHY

In the left column below, list recent incidents with your child that you didn't like. Next, fill in the middle column with assumptions you've made about your child *(she's just doing it to be difficult, he's always the one who breaks things, she never shares…)*. Finally, look over the behavior examples you listed once again, but this time set your intention to "chase the why." Take the time to consider alternate reasons your child could have been behaving the way she was *(she'd had a bad day at school, she was overwhelmed, she was jealous of her baby sister…)*. We've started the exercise off with an example, then add your own in the rows that follow.

WHAT HAPPENED	ASSUMPTION	CHASE THE WHY
When told that she's coming along to have dinner with another family who has "a child just her age," your child: • Says she wants to stay home. • Then throws a fit when you don't back down. • Once there, she refuses to play with the other child, barely even acknowledging her presence.	• She always wants to get her way. • She can't take no for an answer. • She's trying to punish us for making her come to dinner by being rude to us and to our friends. • She doesn't like our friend's child.	I remember that the last time we tried a "blind date" play date it went really poorly, so… • Maybe she's anxious this could be a repeat of that bad experience. • Or, she could be worried that the other child might not like her. • Maybe her own "shark music" is making her fearful. • Maybe she doesn't know how to make play dates successful.

Keep in mind that whatever our children do, they are looking to get their needs met. So we want to avoid making quick assumptions, and instead chase the why so we can get to the root cause of the behavior. *And focusing on the cause (the unmet need), as opposed to the symptoms (the unwanted behavior), is what results in less need for discipline in the long run.*

CONNECTION PRINCIPLE #3 — THINK ABOUT THE HOW

What we say to our kids is, of course, important. But just as important, maybe even more so, is *how* we say it. Therefore, getting some insight into how you're perceived by your children is incredibly valuable as a parent.

When you and your kids have some time alone, and the mood is one of relaxed connection, ask them if you can talk to them about your typical "how." Ask them to give you feedback based on the tone you use when you discipline, when they do something you're not happy with, when they make a mistake. Remember, kindness and respect can—and should—go with clear and consistent discipline. After talking to your kids, answer these questions:

- What did you like hearing from your kids about the way you discipline?

  _____

  _____

  _____

  _____

- What about their experience of the way you communicate was hard for you to hear?

  _____

  _____

  _____

  _____

- If you have more than one child, did they both/all have similar experiences of your "how"?

  _____

  _____

  _____

  _____

- If not, why do you think that is?

  _____

  _____

  _____

  _____

- How can you use this information to improve the aspects of your "how" that you'd like to change?

  _____

  _____

  _____

  _____

It's the *how* that determines what our children feel about us and themselves, and what they learn about treating others. Plus, the *how* goes a long way toward determining their response in the moment, and how successful we'll be at helping produce an effective outcome that makes everyone happier.

THE NO-DRAMA CONNECTION CYCLE

When it comes to connecting with our kids so they *feel felt* and know that we're there to support them, even in the midst of the discipline process, it's helpful for parents to think about connection as a four-part, cyclical process—as illustrated below.

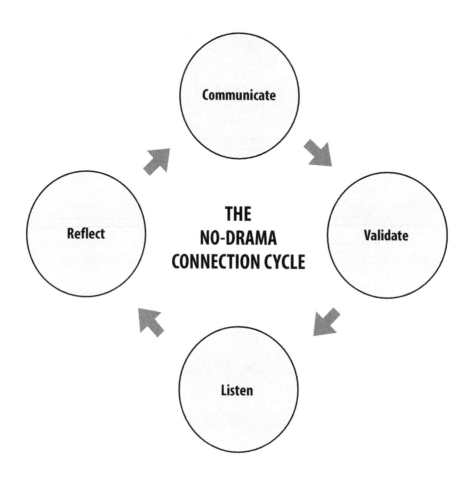

CONNECTION STRATEGY #1 — COMMUNICATE COMFORT

To convey the empathy and connection your child needs so he can calm down enough for learning to take place, you need to communicate that you're not a threat. Then your child's reactive, act-before-thinking downstairs brain can quiet down and he can better process information and regulate his behavior.

Because a child who feels threatened will shift into defense mode to protect himself—which is counterproductive to your goal of teaching him a new skill and then reducing unwanted behavior—taking a deeper look at what you're communicating when you interact with your kids can make a big difference in how they respond.

You've already gained insight about the way your children perceive your *how*. Next, let's take it a step further and consider what you could be doing that they might read as threatening. Use the space provided to answer the questions below.

How often do you think your kids see you as threatening?

o Almost never

o Occasionally

o Often

o Nearly every time I get upset with them

In what ways do you think you make them feel that way *(raising your voice, shaming language, intimidating posture…)*?

_____

_____

_____

How often do you attempt to address a discipline issue when your child is already upset?

o Almost never

o Occasionally

o Often

o Nearly always

How effective does that approach seem to be?

_____

_____

_____

Think about the nonverbal communication you use. Picture yourself when you're really angry. Maybe even think about someone, or something, that upsets you right now. Now describe below what signs your body shows that you're angry *(clenched teeth, crossed arms, hands on hips, frowning…)*?

_____

_____

_____

NONVERBALS ARE POWERFUL...

NONVERBAL MESSAGE: I'M EXASPERATED. YOU WEAR ME OUT. I CAN'T STAND YOU RIGHT NOW. AND I BLAME YOU FOR MAKING THINGS SO HARD ON ME.

NONVERBAL MESSAGE: I AM FURIOUS WITH YOU AND COULD EXPLODE AT ANY MOMENT. BE AFRAID, VERY AFRAID. THIS IS HOW PEOPLE ACT WHEN YOU DO SOMETHING WRONG.

NONVERBAL MESSAGE: YOU'D BETTER DO WHAT I SAY AND NOW! I DON'T CARE HOW YOU FEEL OR WHAT THE CIRCUMSTANCES ARE. POWER, CONTROL, AND AGGRESSION ARE HOW I GET WHAT I WANT.

What about when you're feeling calm and relaxed? What type of nonverbal communication do you send your children *(gentle touches, leaning in with eye contact, smiles...)* ?

_____

_____

NONVERBALS ARE POWERFUL...

WHAT YOU'RE SHARING WITH ME RIGHT NOW IS CRUCIAL — MORE IMPORTANT THAN ANYTHING GOING ON AROUND US, EVEN MORE IMPORTANT THAN ANYTHING I WANT TO SAY.

I KNOW YOU HAD A HARD DAY AT SCHOOL, AND ALTHOUGH I DON'T HAVE JUST THE RIGHT WORDS TO SAY, I'LL ALWAYS BE HERE FOR YOU.

I THINK YOU'RE FANTASTIC, AND YOU FILL ME WITH JOY. I'M NOT EXACTLY HAPPY ABOUT THE DECISION YOU MADE, BUT I LOVE YOU EVEN WHEN YOU MESS UP.

Communicating Comfort By Getting Below Eye Level

In order to get a sense how much of a difference nonverbal communication makes when working through a discipline challenge with your child, in this next exercise you'll be using the "below eye level" technique that communicates "I'm not a threat." By lowering your body so that you're *below* eye level with your child, as well as in a relaxed position, you automatically appear less threatening to her. You communicate safety and comfort to her primitive downstairs brain. Some parents might also add placing a palm to their heart while offering soothing words like, "You really are having such a hard time right now." Finding a way that helps reduce your own tension, in addition to comforting your child, can make it easier for you to offer the connection your child needs when she's upset.

COMMUNICATE COMFORT BY GETTING BELOW EYE LEVEL

The next time your child is having a difficult time controlling her behavior, try the "below eye level" technique and pay attention to any changes you notice *(her reaction, how you felt, what the outcome was…).* Afterwards, return to this page and write down the details of your experience here.

_____

_____

_____

_____

Without ever saying a word, there's so much we express to our children through our body language. Because it's so easy for kids to misinterpret these signals and become upset, it's even more important that we work at being intentional about the messages we send through our nonverbal communication.

CONNECTION STRATEGY #2 — VALIDATE, VALIDATE, VALIDATE

The key to connection when our kids are reactive or making bad choices is validation. In addition to communicating comfort, we need to let our kids know that we hear them. That we understand. That we get it. When we resist the impulse to minimize what our children are going through, we let them know that their feelings matter and are worth paying attention to.

INSTEAD OF DISMISSING...

VALIDATE

While most of us know better than to directly tell our kids that they shouldn't be upset, we've all had moments when we inadvertently give our child the impression that the way she feels is ridiculous or inconvenient. In doing so, we end up invalidating our child's experience of his world.

In the chart below, we've listed a series of scenarios your child might experience. After reading each example, fill in the middle row with an example of an invalidating response and then an example of a validating response in the right-hand column.

WHAT HAPPENED	INVALIDATING RESPONSE	VALIDATING RESPONSE
Your child throws a tantrum because the shirt he wanted to wear to school is in the laundry.		
Your child gets very angry with you when you won't let her go a movie her friends are seeing.		
Your child fell off his skateboard at the park and refuses to try skateboarding again.		
Your child won't eat her sandwich because you cut it diagonally instead of horizontally.		
Your child says he's scared of monsters in his bedroom and keeps getting out of bed after lights out.		

Regardless of how irrational you may feel your child is being in the moment, it's important to remember that the experience is very real and very true *for her*. In offering validation, you're showing that child that you accept her experience of her world and that she can trust you to support her even at her worst.

CONNECTION STRATEGY #3 — STOP TALKING AND LISTEN

Is there a chance that, when your child is upset, you might tend to talk too much? Do you ever over-explain and go all left-brained on your child, instead of really tuning in and hearing what he's feeling? Using the scale below, circle the point that corresponds most closely with how often you find yourself slipping into this mode.

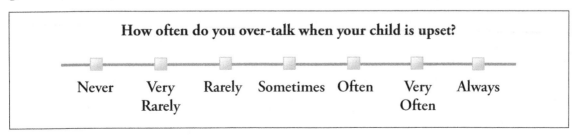

How often do you over-talk when your child is upset?

Never   Very Rarely   Rarely   Sometimes   Often   Very Often   Always

Think back now to a recent example of your child having a hard time. Replay the scene in your mind, remembering as many details as possible: what began the incident, how you spoke, your body language, what you said to your child, her reactions, how you felt when the exchange was over. Take a minute to sit with those memories. Then, as if you're writing one of those choose-your-own-adventure books where making a few different choices leads you to an alternate ending, run through this same memory again except this time come up with a moment or two where you could have listened instead of talked. How do you think your child's responses might have changed?

_____

_____

_____

_____

Because an upset child is already on sensory overload, when you continue to talk, all you're doing is making him more dysregulated and more overwhelmed. And when a child is in that state, he's unable to learn or even hear you. This isn't the time to lecture or defend yourself; this is the time to listen, comfort, and let your child express himself.

CONNECTION STRATEGY #4 — REFLECT WHAT YOU HEAR

The fourth step of the connection cycle is to reflect back to our children what they've said, letting them know we've heard them. If you're not used to doing this, it may feel a bit awkward or unnatural at first. So, take the time now to brainstorm a bit on how to make this process fit for you. What works for one person may feel corny to someone else. What are ways you can let your child know you hear her feelings? What phrases can you use when your child comes to you crying or needs to connect with you for some reason? List three examples.

1. _____

2. _____

3. _____

This type of calm, focused attention on a child who's in the midst of a tantrum or meltdown may seem counter-intuitive to some parents who are more inclined to ignore an upset child to avoid "giving attention to the problem."

But the notion that a child who's displaying unwanted behavior is only doing it for attention deserves a closer look, since this mindset gets in the way of offering the comfort and connection kids need to help them calm down. So ask yourself a few questions.

- Is it normal for kids to seek their parents' attention?
    - o Yes
    - o No

- Do most kids do it?
    - o Yes
    - o No

- When your child tries to get your attention, what do you think she really wants?

_____

_____

_____

_____

It's not only "normal" for a child to want his parents to notice him and pay attention to him, it's actually completely developmentally appropriate. Your child needs your attention to help him regain control, and he doesn't lose control in order to get your attention. Upset kids are going to look toward their closest support system (their parents) to give them the emotional and relational support they need when they are the most dysregulated.

Loving, effective discipline always begins with connection. When we turn down the shark music, chase the why, and pay attention to the how, we can use The No-Drama Connection Cycle to communicate comfort, validate, listen to and reflect our children's feelings. As a result we can create the kind of connection that clearly communicates our love and prepares our children for redirection—which is the focus of the next chapter.

CHAPTER 5

1-2-3 Discipline: Redirecting for Today, and for Tomorrow

> *As kids learn about right and wrong, they also need to learn that life is not just about external reward and punishment. Most important is for children to understand the lesson at hand with as much personal insight as they are developmentally capable of; to empathize with anybody they've hurt; then figure out how to respond to the situation and prevent it in the future.*
>
> *– No-Drama Discipline*

The focus in the last chapter was on connecting and being emotionally responsive to our kids as a means of gaining short-term cooperation and building their brains in the long run. Now we turn to redirection, which is often what people mean when they talk about discipline. We'll explain the basics of redirection by talking about 1-2-3 Discipline focusing on: one definition, two principles, and three desired outcomes.

1-DEFINITION:
Discipline is About Teaching

2-PRINCIPLES:
Wait Until Your Child is Ready

2-PRINCIPLES:
Be Consistent, Not Rigid

3-OUTCOMES:
Insight

3-OUTCOMES:
Empathy

3-OUTCOMES:
Integration and the Repair of Ruptures

Don't worry about memorizing every single idea we'll cover here. We're just offering you an organizing framework to help you focus on what matters as you redirect, and as you discipline, your kids. Keep in mind as you work through this chapter that your discipline will be a lot more successful if you spend less time commanding and demanding, and more time appealing to the upstairs brain.

ONE DEFINITION

Remember, despite what you hear from many people, discipline is not about punishment. It's about teaching. As we explain in the intro of *No-Drama Discipline,* the word "discipline" comes directly from the Latin word *disciplina*, which was used as far back as the 11th century to mean teaching, learning, and giving instruction. So, from its inception in the English language, "discipline" has meant "to teach."

Here's the basic idea: When it comes to discipline moments, having collaborative problem-solving discussions with our kids gives them the opportunity to examine their actions *for themselves* and come to their own conclusions about their behavior. Then they can more deeply understand the ethics and morality of the situations they're faced with, which ultimately leads to the ability to process all of their experiences with that skill set.

So let's start there. When you look back at times you recently disciplined your child, how much of the focus would you say was on teaching or building skills, as opposed to consequences or punishing?

Circle your answer below.

- All
- Most
- Some
- None

What differences might there have been if you had tried to focus on teaching and skill-building, and collaboratively solve the issues at hand? How might this sort of conversation changed the outcome?

_____

_____

_____

_____

_____

_____

The more we give kids the opportunity to consider not only their own desires, but also the desires of others, and practice making good choices that positively impact the people around them, the better they'll be at doing so.

TWO PRINCIPLES

Once we remind ourselves that teaching is our goal, we can be guided by the two principles that make up the next part of 1-2-3 Discipline. These principles ultimately encourage cooperation from your kids and make life easier for both you and them.

PRINCIPLE #1 — WAIT UNTIL YOUR CHILD IS READY

Remember, connection moves a child from reactivity to receptivity. The brain is either in a receptive state or in a reactive state, and we can only learn when we are in a receptive state. So once you've helped your child calm down enough that she's ready to listen and use her upstairs brain, you can redirect. *But there's no point in trying to redirect a child who isn't ready to learn.*

Although we may know that a dysregulated child isn't capable of learning, in the heat of the moment it can be hard for many of us to remember. Do you ever find yourself trying to teach or redirect your child when she's just not ready to hear you? Have you noticed yourself trying to discipline your child when she's so dysregulated that she's out of control and literally unable to hear you or to remain calm and learn?

Why do you think you've done that? Respond to these questions here:

_____

_____

_____

_____

The most effective way to redirect your child's behavior is to wait until he's calm, alert, and receptive. Knowing the signs that your child is too upset to listen and learn can keep you from making the mistake of jumping in at the wrong time.

So let's focus on those signs. Think back to some recent moments when your child was upset. Can you describe any evidence he showed that he was becoming uncomfortable, agitated, or overwhelmed before he became completely dysregulated? Maybe he was breathing heavy, or furrowing his brow, or tensing up his muscles, or turning red, or shaking, or insisting that *of course* he's calm.

List some of your child's main signs that let you know that he's dysregulated, or heading in that direction:

1. _____

2. _____

3. _____

4. _____

Now compare those signs to what you see when your child is calm again. Maybe a relaxed posture or facial expression, an openness to physical contact, a soft voice? Detail that list here.

1. _____

2. _____

3. _____

4. _____

What we want to do is to find that sweet spot for teaching – where you know your child is ready to hear, ready to learn, ready to understand. Every child is different, so becoming aware of what works best for your individual child is key to getting the learning to stick.

At this point make another list, this time of steps you might take to do a better job of waiting to try to teach a lesson until your child is most able to learn. That might involve waiting until later in the day to come back to the issue, or talking about the incident while busy doing something else, or bringing it up when you're both relaxed and cuddling at bedtime. List some ideas here of ways you can wait to teach the lesson until your child is ready to learn it.

1. _____

2. _____

3. _____

4. _____

Keep in mind, too, that your child isn't the only one who needs to be ready. *You* also need to be able to respond to behavior in a way that's not counterproductive. When you're triggered or emotionally overwhelmed you're much more likely to use words or a tone of voice that makes things worse. Like your child, you are either in a receptive or reactive state. We should only teach when we're in a receptive state.

So, what are signs that *you're* not ready? What signals highlight the fact that you're in a reactive, non-receptive state? Is it the way your body feels (*tight jaw, balled fists, clenching stomach*)? Or maybe there are certain things you notice yourself thinking that make you realize you're too worked up – or too exhausted – to be talking to your kids right then (*he's making me insane, what is wrong with her, why do I have to deal with this again…*). Whatever your warning signs are, list them here. Being consciously aware of them is the first step to heeding them.

1. _____

2. _____

3. _____

4. _____

Lastly, what do you do once you've realized that you're not going to be able to discipline in a productive way? Being able to verbalize your feelings not only brings your upstairs brain online and calms your reactive lower brain, it also models the type of behavior you want your child to show when she's upset. So, what can you say to your children to let them know that you need time to calm down before you can continue? Think about what you'd like to communicate to them in that moment. In *No-Drama Discipline* we offered the example of saying, "I'd like to wait until we're really able to talk and listen to each other. We'll come back and talk about it in a while." Write down some possible phrases that would feel natural to you.

1. _____

2. _____

3. _____

4. _____

Being able to read both your child's state of mind, as well as your own—especially during heated moments—means diminishing the drama that comes from trying to force an upset child to obey your commands. Staying connected in this way means discipline will not only be more effective, but will also feel better for both you and your child.

PRINCIPLE #2 — BE CONSISTENT, BUT NOT RIGID

RIGID

Being consistent means that our children know what's expected of them and what to expect from us. It doesn't mean blindly following set rules no matter the circumstances.

Consistency allows for flexibility when the situation calls for it—like skipping bath time tonight because you got home much too late from Grandma's and we're all so tired—and this response comes as a result of thoughtful consideration on our part. Rigidity, on the other hand, often stems from the fear that letting go one time will lead to a slippery slope where our kids never again do as they're told.

CONSISTENT BUT FLEXIBLE

Think about how fear becomes rigidity in your own parenting. What do you worry will become bad habits for your child if you relax your rules (*not letting your small child sleep with you for fear of creating bad sleep habits, enforcing homework-after-school rules without exception, insistence on your child finishing all the food put on his plate…*)?

Fill in the space below with your list of worries that prevent you from being flexible when it comes to rules and boundaries.

_____

_____

_____

_____

Although rigidity is never the goal, there will always be some non-negotiables when it comes to your family. Everyone's list is different; perhaps yours includes having everyone stay at the dinner table until the whole family has finished eating. Someone else might be less concerned about that, but feel that sending handwritten thank-you notes after birthday parties is something they won't compromise on. Whatever your list includes, write some examples here. What are some of your non-negotiables?

_____

_____

_____

_____

So those are priorities you don't want to give on. But there are plenty of times to remain *consistent but flexible*. If you're unsure whether it's OK to be flexible about something, it can help to remember that your ultimate goal is teaching. If flexibility will teach your child more skills than rigidly holding on to a rule, you have your answer.

Look at these typical kid behaviors. After reading through them, decide which ones would go in your non-negotiable category, and which ones, depending on circumstances, would end up in your negotiable category. Put a check next to any negotiables, and an X next to anything you definitely won't budge on. Feel free to add things to this list.

- ❑ Watching TV/Video while eating
- ❑ Drinking soda
- ❑ Playing video games before homework
- ❑ Staying up past bedtime
- ❑ Having sweets more than once in a day
- ❑ Using the computer in a private space (like the bedroom)
- ❑ Name calling *(stupid, dummy, fart face…)*
- ❑ Missing team practice
- ❑ Canceling already agreed-upon plans
- ❑ Excluding someone from a party invitation
- ❑ Refusing to share a toy
- ❑ Lying
- ❑ Sleeping in parents' bed
- ❑ Excluding sibling from play
- ❑ Skipping vegetables at meal times
- ❑ Buckling seat belts in the car
- ❑ Riding the bike without a helmet
- ❑ Walking to a friend's house alone
- ❑ Choosing their own clothes
- ❑ Watching a movie that's rated above their age range
- ❑ Spending extra time playing video games
- ❑ Eating snacks between meals
- ❑ Eating anywhere besides the table
- ❑ Quitting an extracurricular activity
- ❑ Doing homework immediately after school

Did anything surprise you about your choices? Did you expect to find more behaviors on your non-negotiable list than you did? Or vice versa? Many parents find that when they really think about it there are plenty of times to remain consistent but flexible, and this often relieves them of the pressure of feeling that they have to remain rigid in order for their children to be disciplined.

Again, it comes down to response flexibility, rather than offering a rigid, one-size-fits-all response to every discipline situation. It's the response flexibility that allows you to use discipline to help children develop empathy, problem-solving skills, and self-control.

INSTEAD OF RIGIDLY COMMANDING AND DEMANDING...

GIVE HIM PRACTICE DOING THE RIGHT THING

Below you'll see that we've given you some common examples of discipline scenarios. After reading them, fill in the space next to each example with a response that would help your child build whatever skills she may be lacking. We've given you an example on the first one.

DISCIPLINE MOMENT	SKILL-BUILDING RESPONSE
Your older child has a friend over and won't let your younger child play with the friend.	Before the next play date, ask compassion-building questions ("Why do you think it bothers your brother when he doesn't get to play?") and try to problem-solve together ("How could we work it so your brother has some time with you two, and you also have some time away from him?").
Your child makes faces, whines, and nags at you when you won't buy her a toy she wants.	
After not playing as well as he'd hoped at the baseball game, your child complains repeatedly about how unfair the coach is, how the other players cheated, and how he's a much better player than the other kid who got the MVP award.	
You find out that your child hasn't been turning in her homework even though she's been telling you that she has.	

Skill building is a huge part of what discipline is all about. And that requires repeated flexibility and consistency, so you can offer your kids just what they need in each individual situation.

THREE MINDSIGHT OUTCOMES

We've looked at one definition (teaching) and two principles (wait until your child is ready, and be consistent but not rigid) involved in No-Drama Discipline. Now let's look at the three outcomes we're looking to achieve when we redirect.

You'll remember that mindsight is about the ability to see one's own mind, as well as the mind of others. The three outcomes of a successful disciplinary interaction all depend on a healthy dose of mindsight.

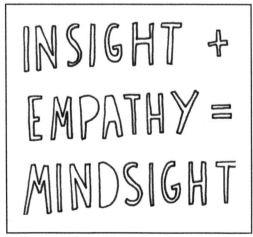

OUTCOME #1 — INSIGHT

Instead of simply commanding and demanding that our kids meet our expectations, parents who follow a *No-Drama Discipline* approach ask their kids to notice and reflect on their own feelings and their responses to difficult situations. Doing this leads your child toward developing personal mindsight. The next chapter will talk more about specific suggestions for building insight in your kids, but for now think about how much you make this a priority when you discipline. In what ways are you actively helping your child develop insight into her own emotions and behaviors? Write down any specific language, actions, or examples here.

_____

_____

_____

_____

Every time we give our children the opportunity to look at their own emotional experience, they have a chance to deepen their self-understanding. And the more they understand *why* they feel the way they do, the more easily they can be mollified and redirected.

OUTCOME #2 — EMPATHY

In addition to helping our kids understand their own feelings, we want to give them lots of practice reflecting on how their actions impact others, seeing things from another's point of view, and developing an awareness of others' feelings. In other words, we want to help them develop their *empathy*.

Think about times your child has been upset about something lately. Write down the details of a few of these interactions in the column on the left, below. When you focus on those discipline moments, do you think you could have used those opportunities to build empathy by asking questions like the ones in these illustrations? Imagining you could go back to those moments of upset again, write the empathy-building questions you would have asked in the right-hand column below.

DISCIPLINE MOMENT	EMPATHY-BUILDING QUESTIONS

The more we give our kids practice considering how someone else feels or experiences a situation, the more empathic and caring they become.

Then, once a child has begun to develop personal insight as well as empathy, it sets the stage for integration—an increased sense of morality and an awareness that he's part of something more than just himself.

OUTCOME #3 — INTEGRATION AND REPAIR OF RUPTURES

After asking our kids to consider their own feelings and then reflect on how their actions impacted others, we want to ask them what they can do to create integration as they repair the situation and make things right. Helping your child realize how her behaviors and actions affect not only herself or another person, but also the relationship between them, is the beginning of her understanding the importance of "we."

Part of teaching your children about the importance of reestablishing connection is helping them understand what's necessary once we've hurt someone—apologizing, yes, but also taking action to address not only the situation their behavior has impacted, but also the other person and, ultimately, the relationship itself.

One way to do this is to work with your children on a physical version of what Dan refers to as Mindsight Maps.

Mindsight Maps: An Exercise

First, collect the following:

- 3-8.5" x 11" sheets of medium weight paper (like construction paper) per person. You can cut these pages down if you wish, but don't go any smaller than 6" x 6".
- Any type of fast drying glue or double-sided tape
- Scissors
- A pile of old magazines that you don't mind being cut up
- Photographs of your child and another person with whom your child has recently experienced conflict. It can be you, a teammate, a sibling, or anyone else your child has a current disconnection from.

To begin, explain to your child the purpose of this exercise: to help him think about the conflict he's recently experienced with his friend or sibling.

Then explain that his first task is to create a sheet of paper that represents him. He can call this his "me" page, and it will represent who he is. Next, sift through the magazines and photographs with your child to cut out words, phrases, and pictures that he feels best represent himself. Glue these onto the "me" page.

Do your best to let your child choose the descriptions; it will give you some insight into how he views himself. However, if you notice he needs a nudge to recognize certain qualities, feel free to make some gentle suggestions. Not every child feels comfortable saying that they're brave, nor is every child aware that they can be easily hurt.

Now create a similar page about the other person, the one your child has experienced conflict with. This will be your child's "you" page.

When both pages are complete, take a moment to step back to look at them and, together with your child, reflect on what he's made. Here are some example prompts you can use, but feel free to ask whatever questions seem appropriate to you:

- Was there anything surprising that came up for you as you made these pages?
- I notice that you described yourself as _____ (choose something that stands out for you). Can you tell me more about that?
- Is there anything about your "me" page that you think _____ (the other person) would be surprised to see?
- If so, do you think not knowing that about you had anything to do with the conflict you had?
- Alternately, do you think if _____ had known that about you anything would have changed?
- Do you think _____ would be surprised with any part of the "you" page you made?
- I notice that you use _____ to describe _____ (the other person). Can you tell me more about that?

After this discussion, create with your child a third page, the "we" page. Explain that you'll be using the same method of cutting words, phrases and pictures from magazines to fill that sheet of paper. For the "we" page, though, he should concentrate on depicting the relationship between himself and the other person *before* the disconnection occurred.

Once the "we" page is complete, ask your child to think about the relationship, and about how the "me" and the "you" join to become a "we." Let it sink in for your child that, despite the recent conflict, a strong relationship exists between the "me" and the "you."

Then, while looking at the "we" page, you can lead your child towards thinking about repairing that relationship. You may need to direct your child a bit, but the more he can come up with his own ideas, the more he'll be able to take ownership of his role. Some helpful prompts could include the following:

- What do you think _____ (the other person) was thinking when _____ (the incident) happened?
- How do you think that made her feel?
- How do you feel about your relationship with _____ right now?
- What would you want *her* to do to make things better if the roles were reversed?
- What you think she would need from *you* to repair the situation?
- How would it make you feel to do that?

Sometimes your child may feel that the other person is primarily (or solely) to blame. Use that admission as a chance to explain how *both* parties have a role in restoring connection—even if all one side needs to do is extend understanding, forgiveness, or a release of blame. Remind your child that all he needs to concentrate on is what actions *he* can take.

Making these physical representations of your child's relationships helps to bring often-subconscious thoughts, feelings, and emotions to the surface—allowing children to deepen their ability to know themselves, consider the feelings of others, and take action toward repairing a situation. All of this gives kids the opportunity to build and strengthen the connections within the frontal lobe, resulting in understanding themselves better and being able to get along with others as they move into adolescence and adulthood.

As we end this chapter, take a moment to look back at the different aspects we've discussed and think about what the most challenging areas seem to be for you. Maybe you want to get more practice with collaborative problem solving, or more consistently find your child's "sweet spot" for learning, or respond to discipline moments more regularly with empathy building questions. Whatever it might be, choose what you'd like to focus on first and come up with an action step you can take right away. Write the details of your plan here.

_____

_____

_____

_____

_____

_____

By reminding yourself about the definition and purpose of discipline, the principles that guide it, and your desired outcomes, you'll give yourself a much better chance of disciplining your kids—of teaching them—in a way that leads to more cooperation from them and better relationships among all members of the family.

CHAPTER 6

Addressing Behavior: As Simple as R-E-D-I-R-E-C-T

Don't underestimate how powerful a kind tone of voice can be as you initiate a conversation about the behavior you're wanting to change. Remember that, ultimately, you're trying to remain firm and consistent in your discipline while still interacting with your child in a way that communicates warmth, love, respect, and compassion. These two aspects of parenting can and should coexist.

– No-Drama Discipline

This chapter will focus on giving you specific strategies for redirection. But first, let's remind ourselves of a few key "pre-redirection" principles that guide a No-Drama discipline approach:

- All effective discipline begins with connection.
- Remember to pause a moment before immediately launching into a reactive discipline mode.
- Ask yourself, "Is my child ready to learn right now?"
- Ask yourself, "Am I ready?"

Responding to discipline situations with this level of attunement and respect makes all the difference when it comes to how events play out. But it's not always easy. Which principles on the list do you think you need to work on the most?

- Connecting first
- Pausing before immediately launching into a reactive discipline mode
- Waiting until your child is ready
- Waiting until *you* are ready

Now, think about how you could increase your skill with the aspect you chose. What would you need to do? Is there anyone who could help you? Can you think of any recent examples where you more successfully achieved this goal? What made the difference for you in those circumstances? Write your thoughts here, then we'll focus more specifically on redirection strategies.

_____

_____

_____

_____

STRATEGIES TO HELP YOU R-E-D-I-R-E-C-T

You'll recall that we've arranged the No-Drama redirection strategies into an acronym.

Reduce words

Embrace emotions

Describe, don't preach

Involve your child in the discipline

Reframe a no into a conditional yes

Emphasize the positive

Creatively approach the situation

Teach mindsight tools

Remember, this isn't a list you need to memorize or a plan to rigidly adhere to. Rather, these recommendations should be a part of your parenting toolbox—strategies and approaches from which you can choose depending on the circumstances, your children's ages, their temperaments, their developmental stages, and your own parenting philosophy.

REDIRECTION STRATEGY #1 — <u>R</u>EDUCE WORDS

When disciplining, parents often feel compelled to lecture about what their children have done wrong, or how they can do things better next time. Resisting the urge to overtalk when you redirect actually gives the words you do use greater value.

WHAT A PARENT SAYS:

WHAT THE CHILD HEARS:

Keeping that point in mind, use the following scale to rate how often you overtalk during discipline moments.

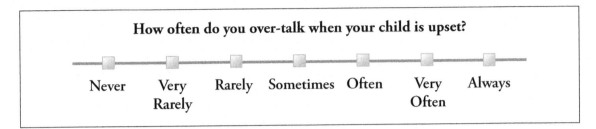

How often do you over-talk when your child is upset?

Never　Very　Rarely　Sometimes　Often　Very　Always
　　　　Rarely　　　　　　　　　　　Often

As we discuss in *No-Drama Discipline*, too much talking is counterproductive—especially with a toddler. As you can see from the illustrated example below, addressing your child's actions and then immediately moving on lets you avoid giving the negative behavior too much attention and quickly gets you back on track.

ADDRESSING TODDLER MISBEHAVIOR IN FOUR STEPS

STEP 1: Connect and address the feelings behind the behavior

Step 2: Address the behavior

Step 3: Give alternatives

Step 4: Move on

Think about your own child right now. When you think about the interactions you two share, to what extent does she respond to lots of words? Do you tend to have long back and forth conversation with your child during discipline moments? Does she stay focused throughout, or seem to zone out shortly after you've started speaking?

If you weren't using words, what could be a better approach to take when trying to get a lesson across to your child *(drawing pictures, writing letters back and forth, telling a story with dolls, talking during an activity like riding bikes or throwing a ball...)* ? Write about your ideas here.

_____

_____

_____

_____

The next time your child is behaving in a way you don't like, choose one of the alternative approaches you wrote about here to try with him. Then come back here to make notes about the results.

_____

_____

_____

_____

REDIRECTION STRATEGY #2 — EMBRACE EMOTIONS

It's important to remember that feelings are neither good nor bad, neither valid nor invalid. Feelings just *are*. Helping our children navigate what they *do* with those feelings is what we, as parents, want to focus on.

As we put it in No-Drama Discipline, "We want our kids to believe at a deep level that even as we teach them about right and wrong behavior, their feelings and experiences will always be validated and honored. When kids feel this from their parents even during redirection, they'll be much more apt to learn the lessons the parents are teaching, meaning that over time, the overall number of disciplinary moments will decrease."

For many parents it feels really difficult to be OK with their children experiencing negative emotions. For some parents, accepting that their child has big feelings—especially unpleasant ones—feels as though they're accepting poor behavior. For others, negative emotions may trigger unpleasant childhood memories of their own. Whatever your own experience is with expressing feelings, learning to embrace your child's emotions is an integral part of connecting with her.

Think now, about how comfortable you actually are when your child expresses big emotions. What reactions do you have when she's furious, when she says she hates someone, when she seems despondent, or when she's anxious? How does your body feel? What thoughts come up for you? Below you'll see a list of behaviors that can indicate discomfort. Circle the ones that you've noticed you exhibit.

- Suppressing emotions *(stop crying, don't be upset, don't be nervous...)*
- Having your buttons pushed *(your child's emotions make you feel angry, irritated, burdened...)*
- Tuning out
- Rushing your child to "get over it"

- Downplaying the emotion *(you're overreacting, how can you be angry about that, it's not a big deal…)*
- Denying the emotions
- Trying to "spin" the problem *(you're better off now, it's for the best, there must be a reason this happened…)*
- Mocking/making fun
- Labeling *(you're so shy, you're being too sensitive, you're so rude…)*
- Diverting attention
- Blaming the child *(if you had listened, that wouldn't have happened)*

This is by no means a complete list, but it should give you some insight into your own feelings about emotions. When you notice yourself exhibiting any of these behaviors, or feeling uncomfortable in any way when your child is upset, try chasing the why for your own behavior. Get to the bottom of *why* you're uncomfortable, so you can ultimately be able to embrace all of your child's emotions—not just the happy ones.

INSTEAD OF SQUELCHING EMOTIONS...

SAY YES TO THE FEELINGS AND NO TO THE BEHAVIOR

Below, we've given you a series of hypothetical discipline situations. For each description, come up with a response that would allow you to embrace your child's emotions while still addressing the behavior and setting limits. Use the illustration on the previous page as an example of what we mean.

DISCIPLINE SITUATION	RESPONSE
Your child complains about having to clean up her room – especially the part of the mess her friend made when she had a play date over.	
Your child won't compromise with his brother to choose an activity they can do together.	
You find out that your child is playing video games you told him he wasn't allowed to play.	

Acknowledging your kids' feelings during redirection benefits them in many ways, including calming and regulating their nervous system, priming them to be able to easily learn whatever lesson you want to teach, and reminding them that—even at their worst—their parents will honor and respect him.

REDIRECTION STRATEGY #3 — DESCRIBE, DON'T PREACH

When faced with unwanted behavior, many parents find themselves criticizing and lecturing their children about the behaviors they don't approve of. In most instances, a nitpicking or demanding response is not only unnecessary, it also puts your child on the defensive—not a good place to be when it comes to learning anything. However, a response that has you simply *describing* what you notice, helps your child exercise his upstairs brain and increase both his empathy and problem-solving skills, while also setting up a level of mutual respect and trust in the relationship.

INSTEAD OF COMMANDING AND DEMANDING...

DESCRIBE WHAT YOU SEE

INSTEAD OF CRITCIZING AND ATTACKING...

DESCRIBE WHAT YOU ARE SEEING

Look at the following list of statements a parent might make during a discipline moment. After reading through them, cross out the statements that criticize or "command and demand," and circle the ones that simply describe what's going on, leaving it to the child to respond to what she's heard.

- Don't jump on the couch.
- You can't stay up past your bedtime.
- I see your Legos are all out.
- You're frustrated because Amelia wants to go to the beach, but you wanted to go to her house.
- You didn't make your snack for school and now we're running late.
- It looks like Max wants a turn on the trampoline.
- Your homework has to be finished before you can go out with your friends.
- It looks like the garbage cans haven't been emptied in a while.
- How could you forget to turn in your homework?
- I see Josie sitting over there while you and Olivia play together.
- Stop yelling at your brother.
- You need to share that with your cousin.
- I see dishes still on the table.
- It looks like the dog needs to go for a walk.
- If you hadn't been running by the pool, you wouldn't have gotten hurt.

Telling kids what they did wrong, lecturing them about "the right way" to accomplish something, and demanding they do as you say, are discipline approaches that may be familiar to you, but they often lead to defensiveness and disconnection. Even toddlers know right from wrong—what kids *actually* need from their parents is the help to recognize bad decisions they're making and what leads up to those decisions, so they can make better choices next time.

REDIRECTION STRATEGY #4 — INVOLVE YOUR CHILD IN THE DISCIPLINE

Many of us grew up in families in which discipline discussions consisted of the parent lecturing the child and the child being expected to dutifully listen to the lecture.

Although this one-directional monologue has long been seen by parents as the most effective way to get their point across, many are learning now that the way to more cooperation, connection, and harmony within the family is a bi-directional approach—a dialogue where parents and kids work *as a team* to find solutions to the problems that created the need for discipline in the first place.

PARENT ⟷ CHILD

INSTEAD OF DELIVERING A MONOLOGUE...

INVOLVE YOUR CHILD IN THE DISCIPLINE

INSTEAD OF COMMANDING AND DEMANDING...

INVOLVE YOUR KIDS IN THE DISCIPLINE

Thinking now about your own child, come up with an example of a disciplinary situation that the two of you face regularly and describe below how you could involve her in solving it *(ask for her ideas on how to make necessary changes, make your suggestion and ask if it works for her as well, discuss what you can both do differently next time...)*

_____

_____

_____

_____

Next, write out what you might say to your child when asking her to help you come up with a better way to solve the problem or address the issue. What words would you use?

_____

_____

_____

_____

When you involve your kids in the discipline process, you not only give them the opportunity to practice reflecting on their behavior as well as helping them develop their self-awareness, you also show how important their input and ideas are to you—thus, deepening the parent-child bond.

REDIRECTION STRATEGY #5 — REFRAME A NO INTO A CONDITIONAL YES

How we say no to our children, and how often we say it, makes a difference in whether our children resist the word, or learn from it. Being able to set boundaries while remaining supportive, respectful, and connected may take reframing the way you look at the point of saying "no." Start by asking yourself how often you find yourself saying "no" to your child throughout the day? On the chart below, circle the answer you think fits bests for you.

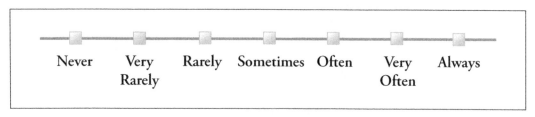

Never   Very Rarely   Rarely   Sometimes   Often   Very Often   Always

Limits are important, but sometimes we don't even have to set them as firmly as we do, or we can do so in different ways. A conditional yes lets you empathize with your child's desires, while giving him practice understanding limits and increasing his tolerance for disappointment and delayed gratification.

Now think back to some recent moments with your child where you told her "no" but could have used a conditional yes. In the left hand column of the following chart, give an example of what your child asked for that you said no to. In the right hand column, write an alternative, conditional yes response that you could have given. For example, instead of "No, we can't go to the park because it's raining," you could say, "I know you really love going to the park. When it stops raining, we can go!"

WHAT YOUR CHILD SAYS	CONDITIONAL YES RESPONSE

Think of your conditional yes as compromising with your child, or saying yes when it works best. This isn't a sign of weakness; rather, it's showing respect and consideration. In addition, you're helping her develop some pretty complex skills—delaying gratification, considering not only what she wants, but also what others want, and then making good arguments based on that information. These skills will benefit her throughout her life.

INSTEAD OF AN OUTRIGHT NO...

REFRAME THE NO INTO A CONDITIONAL YES

REDIRECTION STRATEGY #6 — EMPHASIZE THE POSITIVE

What's your first reaction when someone points out that you've done something wrong? Perhaps you get defensive? Or maybe you feel ashamed? You might even get angry. Feeling motivated to do better is probably not high on your list of emotions at that point. It's the same for our children. When they are behaving in a less than optimal way, it's possible (and more effective) to teach them the lesson or skill they need without making it a negative experience. Instead of pointing out all the things your kids are doing that you dislike, focusing on the parts of their behavior that you *do* like will positively reinforce their desire to repeat those behaviors.

INSTEAD OF FOCUSING ON THE PROBLEM...

EMPHASIZE THE POSITIVE

EMPHASIZE THE POSITIVE BY CATCHING
YOUR KIDS BEHAVING WELL

A lot of us fall into habitual responses when we're frustrated. Sometimes those responses aren't the most positive ones. Maybe you find yourself saying things like, "Knock it off!" or "Quit it!" or "What is wrong with you?" more often than you'd like to admit. When your kids do something you don't like (perhaps for the hundredth time), what are the most typical negative phrases you use? Write a few of them here.

_____

_____

_____

_____

_____

Next, write three of these phrases on three separate index cards. Then, on the backs of the cards, write a positive phrase you want to use instead. Maybe "I like the way you…" or "Let's try that again in a different way" or "It's really helpful when you…."

For the next couple of days, carry these cards with you, and make yourself "flip the card over" when you discipline. Be sure to come back here to make notes about any differences you notice when you're doing this *(how you felt, your child's reactions, the outcome of your interactions…)*.

_____

_____

_____

_____

_____

Involve your children in this approach. Tell them you're working on being more positive, and explain the idea. Then ask them to work with you, and to remind you when they hear you being more negative. Not only does this set a good example and make them a witness to your intention, it may possibly influence the way they interact with their siblings and friends.

REDIRECTION STRATEGY #7 — CREATIVELY APPROACH THE SITUATION

As we've said repeatedly, there's no one-size-fits-all discipline technique that solves every situation. Response flexibility—the ability to think on your feet and to pause and consider different solutions depending on circumstances—is the tool you'll want to rely on most often. Being able to creatively respond to whatever discipline situation crops up is what will help you reduce the drama involved when you don't like the way your kids are acting.

INSTEAD OF COMMANDING AND DEMANDING...

BE CREATIVE AND PLAYFUL

We understand that you don't always have the energy or the inclination to be creative. But think of it this way. You basically have two main options:

Option #1: Be creative about how you respond to your child's behavior. Although it can take more effort than you want to expend in the moment, playfulness and silliness can shift the mood and end the drama quickly, so that everyone involved ends up having fun.

Option #2: Continue with whatever battle or power struggle the discipline situation has created. Keep butting heads until you "win" the power struggle with your child. This option will usually take more time and energy and often results in disconnection and hurt feelings.

Looking at it this way, doesn't Option #1 sound easier? And even though it might seem like more work at first, it's actually a way to avoid escalating drama.

As a way of committing to this idea, take the time to write a note to yourself about why you're going to be creative about your discipline, and how you plan to do it. If it helps, you can start by thinking about specific discipline situations that tend to repeat themselves in your family, then come up with some creative ways you can respond to those specific instances the next time they happen.

_____

_____

_____

_____

_____

REDIRECTION STRATEGY #8 — TEACH MINDSIGHT TOOLS

You'll remember from Chapter 2 that mindsight is all about seeing your own mind, as well as the mind of another. And the more we can do that for our kids, the easier discipline will be. Even more important, they'll continue to grow in their ability to relate well to others and enjoy deep relationships, not to mention dealing with their own feelings and avoiding becoming victims to their surroundings.

Helping our kids develop the personal insight that allows them to understand their own minds and handle difficult situations, sets them on their way to realizing how empowering it is to be able to take charge of how they feel and how they act.

Take a minute now to review the mindsight tools we discussed in Chapter 6 of *No-Drama Discipline* and in Chapter 5 of *The Whole-Brain Child*. We've highlighted a few of them below as well. Which of these—or other mindsight tools you know about yourself—could you teach your kids about right away? Do you see one you could put it into practice this week, or even today?

Going to a peaceful place — *helping kids manage anxieties, frustrations, and anger by teaching them to shift their focus to feelings of calm*

INSTEAD OF 'DISMISS AND DENY'

EXERCISE MINDSIGHT

Narrating the present moment — *teaching children to be actors, experiencing a scene in the moment, but also to be the director, who watches more objectively and can, from outside the scene, be more insightful about what's taking place on camera*

Taking control of upsetting images – *helping kids change the pictures in their minds*

INSTEAD OF 'DISMISS AND DENY'...

TRY USING MINDSIGHT TO TAKE CONTROL OF IMAGES

Using the hand model of the brain – *teaching children to understand and express what happens around and within themselves, so they can then make intentional choices about how to respond*

WHOLE-BRAIN KIDS: Teach Your Kids About Their Downstairs and Upstairs Brain

YOUR DOWNSTAIRS BRAIN AND YOUR UPSTAIRS BRAIN

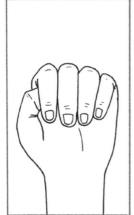

MAKE A FIST WITH YOUR HAND. THIS IS WHAT WE CALL A HAND MODEL OF YOUR BRAIN. REMEMBER HOW YOU HAVE A LEFT SIDE AND A RIGHT SIDE TO YOUR BRAIN? WELL, YOU ALSO HAVE AN UPSTAIRS AND A DOWNSTAIRS PART OF YOUR BRAIN.

THE UPSTAIRS BRAIN IS WHERE YOU MAKE GOOD DECISIONS AND DO THE RIGHT THING, EVEN WHEN YOU ARE FEELING REALLY UPSET.

NOW LIFT YOUR FINGERS A LITTLE BIT. SEE WHERE YOUR THUMB IS? THAT'S PART OF YOUR DOWNSTAIRS BRAIN, AND IT'S WHERE YOUR REALLY BIG FEELINGS COME FROM. IT LETS YOU CARE ABOUT OTHER PEOPLE AND FEEL LOVE. IT ALSO LETS YOU FEEL UPSET, LIKE WHEN YOU'RE MAD OR FRUSTRATED.

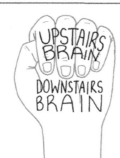

THERE'S NOTHING WRONG WITH FEELING UPSET. THAT'S NORMAL, ESPECIALLY WHEN YOUR UPSTAIRS BRAIN HELPS YOU CALM DOWN. FOR EXAMPLE, CLOSE YOUR FINGERS AGAIN. SEE HOW THE UPSTAIRS THINKING PART OF YOUR BRAIN IS TOUCHING YOUR THUMB, SO IT CAN HELP YOUR DOWNSTAIRS BRAIN EXPRESS YOUR FEELINGS CALMLY?

SOMETIMES WHEN WE GET REALLY UPSET, WE CAN FLIP OUR LID. RAISE YOUR FINGERS LIKE THIS. SEE HOW YOUR UPSTAIRS BRAIN IS NO LONGER TOUCHING YOUR DOWNSTAIRS BRAIN? THAT MEANS IT CAN'T HELP IT STAY CALM.

FOR EXAMPLE:

THIS IS WHAT HAPPENED TO JEFFREY WHEN HIS SISTER DESTROYED HIS LEGO TOWER. HE FLIPPED HIS LID AND WANTED TO SCREAM AT HER.

BUT JEFFREY'S PARENTS HAD TAUGHT HIM ABOUT FLIPPING HIS LID, AND HOW HIS UPSTAIRS BRAIN COULD HUG HIS DOWN-STAIRS BRAIN AND HELP HIM CALM DOWN. HE WAS STILL ANGRY, BUT INSTEAD OF SHOUTING AT HIS SISTER, HE WAS ABLE TO TELL HER HE WAS ANGRY AND ASK HIS PARENTS TO CARRY HER OUT OF HIS ROOM.

SO THE NEXT TIME YOU FEEL YOURSELF STARTING TO FLIP YOUR LID, MAKE A BRAIN MODEL WITH YOUR HAND. (REMEMBER IT'S A BRAIN MODEL, NOT AN ANGRY FIST!) PUT YOUR FINGERS STRAIGHT UP, THEN SLOWLY LOWER THEM SO THAT THEY'RE HUGGING YOUR THUMB. THIS WILL BE YOUR REMINDER TO USE YOUR UPSTAIRS BRAIN TO HELP YOU CALM THOSE BIG FEELINGS IN THE DOWN-STAIRS BRAIN.

Giving kids mindsight tools enables them to regulate their emotions, rather than be ruled by them. The self-awareness and sense of control that this gives our children is a gift that, along with the rest of the *No-Drama Discipline* tools, helps them grow into kind and responsible people who enjoy successful relationships and meaningful lives.

Take a minute now and write about how you'll put one (or more!) of these mindsight tools into practice this week.

_____

_____

_____

_____

_____

Remember, although this chapter contains lots of different ideas and tools you can use, the point isn't to memorize them or to blindly follow a program. Your goal is to be able to flexibly pull out whichever tool seems to fit a particular moment. Then you can create a discipline approach based in connection, instead of drama.

On Magic Wands, Being Human, Reconnection, and Change: Four Messages of Hope

Right now, in this moment, you can commit to giving your children these valuable tools. You can help them develop this increased capacity to regulate themselves, to make good choices, and to handle themselves well — even in challenging times, and even when you're not around.

– No-Drama Discipline

We recognize that even with the best of intentions and approaches, discipline can often be hard on kids, on parents, and on the relationship. So *No-Drama Discipline Workbook* leaves you with four messages of hope.

MESSAGE OF HOPE #1 — THERE IS NO MAGIC WAND

Sometimes, no matter how much we know, nothing we try with our kids is going to be successful. Sometimes they're still going to be angry, they're still going to say they hate us, they're still going to continue to have a hard time. For many parents this is a difficult truth to accept. And some of us just aren't comfortable when we don't succeed with what we set out to do (*cough* Any other perfectionist parents out there?).

How hard is that for you? When you realize that your child is having a hard time, and there's nothing you can do to "fix" things, and she won't acknowledge your attempts to reconnect and respond, to what extent are you able to just be there for her? Is it a struggle for you when you've done your best but your child is still upset? Write out your thoughts.

_____

_____

_____

Sometimes there's no magic wand, but not being able to make things right doesn't make you a bad parent. Sometimes all we can do is communicate our love, give our kids space when they ask for it, be available when they do want us close, and talk about the situation when they're ready.

MESSAGE OF HOPE #2 — YOUR KIDS BENEFIT EVEN WHEN YOU MESS UP

None of us are perfect parents. But many of us have a voice in our heads telling us we should be. For some, this voice is just a reminder to do better next time. But for others it can be a constant, overwhelming, and stressful presence. When you mess up as a parent, how hard are you on yourself? What do you tell yourself? What do you worry about? Write about it here.

_____

_____

_____

Although none of us wants to mess up, there are a number of benefits children *do* get when their parents make mistakes:

- It gives kids opportunities to deal with difficult situations, thus developing new skills.
- Kids have to learn to control themselves even though their parent isn't doing such a great job of controlling herself.
- They get to see you model how to apologize and make things right.
- They experience that when there's conflict and argument, there can be repair, and things can be good again.
- They learn to trust, and even expect, that calm and connection will follow conflict.
- They learn that their actions affect other people's emotions and behavior.
- They see that you're not perfect, so they won't expect themselves to be, either.

Think back now to recent moments where you responded to your children from a less-than-optimal place. Which of the benefits listed above apply most fully to your own situation? In the space below, write about the lessons they've learned from your not-so-great parenting moments.

_____

_____

_____

_____

_____

Abuse is obviously different, and if you're harming your child or the relationship, that's reason enough to seek immediate help. But assuming you're continuing to nurture the relationship and repair it when there's been conflict, you can relax and know that your kids are learning important lessons even when you're not at your best.

MESSAGE OF HOPE #3 — YOU CAN ALWAYS RECONNECT

There's no way to avoid experiencing conflict with your children. It's normal that misunderstandings, arguments, and conflicting agendas will invariably lead to ruptures in the relationship—sometimes multiple times a day. However, it's important to recognize the value in repairing and restoring the connection between parent and child as soon as possible when a rupture does occur.

How hard is it for you to let go of resentment and frustration you feel towards your child when he's done something you didn't want him to do? Do you find yourself holding on to negative thoughts and emotions? Think about recent blow-ups you've had with your child and examine your thoughts and behavior. How difficult was it for you to make repairs? Write about your experience here.

_____

_____

_____

_____

_____

_____

_____

_____

_____

_____

_____

_____

_____

_____

_____

_____

_____

REPAIR A RUPTURE ASAP

The longer we take to make the repairs after a rupture, the more likely it is for negative feelings and associations to fester and grow. Disregarding the need for the repair altogether can be even more hurtful to a child. Although parents may know this on some level, their own feelings and unexamined beliefs about discipline can get in the way of quickly making repairs and lead to prolonged disconnection. When you look at the arguments and breakdowns you've had in your relationships (with your children or with other adults), do you tend to reconnect as soon as possible? Or do you hold grudges, give silent treatments, pretend the ruptures never happened, or other similar behavior? Write about your typical behavior here.

_____

_____

_____

_____

_____

_____

Of course we want to redirect when our kids make poor choices. We want to teach them to behave in socially acceptable ways. But we also want to help them recognize and deal with limits and boundaries, to understand the implications of the decisions they make, and to relate to others with kindness, empathy, and a strong moral compass. It's your relationship with your child that makes all of that possible. So, while correcting behavior is important, it's your relationship that has to come first. If the relationship has experienced a rupture, find a way to make reconnection your priority.

MESSAGE OF HOPE #4 — IT'S NEVER TOO LATE TO MAKE A POSITIVE CHANGE

Even if you feel that your discipline strategy, up until now, has run counter to everything we've discussed in this book, it's never too late to change things for the better. Neuroplasticity, as we've said, shows us that the brain is amazingly changeable and adaptive across a lifetime. As you become more intentional about how you respond to your children, you activate certain circuits in their brains. This circuitry that is repeatedly activated will be strengthened and further developed. (Remember: neurons that fire together, wire together). No matter how long you've been using a discipline strategy that you now feel doesn't work, as soon as you've committed to respond with calm, loving connection, you 3begin to strengthen and develop a reflective, insightful, and regulated upstairs brain not only for your child, but for yourself as well.

As a final exercise, flip back through this book and pull out the three or four main ideas you want to begin putting into action right away. Write out the idea here, along with specific actions steps you can take towards making a positive change in the way you discipline your child.

_____

_____

_____

_____

_____

For many parents, a No-Drama, Whole-Brain approach to discipline means dismantling many long-held beliefs about parenting. For others, it means making just a few shifts in the way they respond to their upset children. Wherever you fall on this spectrum, remember that no one is able to discipline the way they want every time they get the chance. But, if you can remain open to a new way of doing things, make your relationship with your child a priority, and work hard to understand your own reactions and behaviors, you'll be taking great steps towards loving and disciplining your kids in ways that are good for all of you as individuals, and for your whole family.

Acknowledgments

We want to thank PESI for being so supportive throughout the process of publishing this workbook. We especially appreciate Linda Jackson, whose enthusiasm and professionalism, along with a great deal of patience, make her everything we could hope for in an editor.

Also, we gratefully acknowledge Gina Osher for the countless contributions she made to the writing of this book. We appreciate her both personally and professionally, and we thank her for her insightful ideas and creative approaches to finding more and more practical applications of the ideas from No-Drama Discipline.

Finally, we want to thank all the parents, teachers, therapists, and group leaders who have communicated with us through the years, sharing their stories and helping us implement and apply these ideas in ways that let us help more families and kids. We thank all our readers for the ways you've embraced The Whole-Brain Child and No-Drama Discipline, as well as the workbooks that have followed from them. Together we can all continue to raise generations of kids who are happier, healthier, and more fully themselves.

Dan and Tina

About the Authors

Daniel J. Siegel, M.D. is a graduate of Harvard Medical School and completed his postgraduate medical education at UCLA with training in pediatrics and child adolescent, and adult psychiatry. He is currently a clinical professor of psychiatry at the UCLA School of Medicine, founding co-director of UCLA's Mindful Awareness Research Center, and executive director of the Mindsight Institute.

Dr. Siegel's psychotherapy practice spans 25 years and he has authored three *New York Times* bestsellers: *Brainstorm*, and two books with Tina Payne Bryson, Ph.D., *The Whole-Brain Child* and *No-Drama Discipline*. His other books include *Mind: A Journey to the Heart of Being Human*, *Mindsight*, *Pocket Guide to Interpersonal Neurobiology*, *The Developing Mind*, Second Edition, *The Mindful Therapist*, *The Mindful Brain*, and *Parenting from the Inside-Out* (with Mary Hartzell, M.Ed.), and *The Whole-Brain Child Workbook* (with Tina Payne Bryson), and he is the founding editor of the Norton Series on Interpersonal Neurobiology. Dr. Siegel has been invited to lecture for the King of Thailand, Pope John Paul II, His Holiness the Dalai Lama, Google University, and TEDx. www.drdansiegel.com

Dr. Tina Payne Bryson, is a pediatric and adolescent psychotherapist and the Executive Director of the Center for Connection in Pasadena, CA. She is also the co-author (with Dan Siegel) of two *New York Times* bestsellers: *The Whole-Brain Child* and *No Drama-Discipline*, along with *The Whole-Brain Child Workbook*. She keynotes conferences and conducts workshops for parents, educators, and clinicians all over the world. Dr. Bryson earned her Ph.D. from the University of Southern California, and she lives near Los Angeles with her husband and three children. You can learn more about her at www.TinaBryson.com, where you can subscribe to her blog and read her articles about kids and parenting.

Made in the USA
Monee, IL
12 November 2019